CHAMPIONSHIP SWIMMING

How to Improve Your Technique and Swim Faster in Thirty Days or Less

Tracey McFarlane Mirande

with Kathlene Bissell

McGraw·Hill

New York   Chicago   San Francisco   Lisbon   London   Madrid   Mexico City
Milan   New Delhi   San Juan   Seoul   Singapore   Sydney   Toronto

Library of Congress Cataloging-in-Publication Data

McFarlane Mirande, Tracey.
 Championship swimming : how to improve your technique and swim faster in thirty days or less / by Tracey McFarlane Mirande and Kathlene Bissell ; with photos by Ben Van Horn.
  p.   cm.
  ISBN 0-07-144730-X
  1. Swimming—Training.   I. Bissell, Kathlene.   II. Title.

 GV837.7. M34   2005
 797.2'1—dc22   2004030824

To Travis, the light of my life
—TMM

To my daughter, Tamara
—KB

3 4 5 6 7 8 9 0   DOC/DOC   0 9 8 7

ISBN 0-07-144730-X

Interior photos by Ben Van Horn

McGraw-Hill books are available at special quantity discounts to use as premiums and sales promotions, or for use in corporate training programs. For more information, please write to the Director of Special Sales, Professional Publishing, McGraw-Hill, Two Penn Plaza, New York, NY 10121-2298. Or contact your local bookstore.

Consult your physician or health care professional before beginning this, or any, exercise program. Not all exercise programs are suitable for everyone. Discontinue any exercise that causes you discomfort or pain and consult a medical expert. The instructions and advice presented in this book are in no way a substitute for medical counseling. The authors and publisher disclaim any liability arising directly or indirectly from the use of this book.

This book is printed on acid-free paper.

CONTENTS

FOREWORD

Tracey McFarlane Mirande is known as one of the finest breaststrokers in USA Swimming history. She was a 1988 Olympian in Seoul, Korea, and winner of the U.S. Olympic Trials in the 100- and 200-meter breaststroke.

I also know Tracey as a collegiate athlete who won many NCAA championships in breaststroke and participated in many NCAA championship medley relays while she was swimming for and I was coaching at the University of Texas. It was because of Tracey's desire to do everything possible to help her college team be successful that I know she is highly qualified to write this book on improving swimming technique.

When Tracey came to the University of Texas, she was "only a breast-stroker" without a third individual event to enter at the NCAAs. Her first year, we tried the 50-yard freestyle, but she did not qualify for the NCAA championships. Her sophomore year, we tried the 200-yard individual medley, but again she did not qualify for the championships. Her junior year, she qualified for the championships but did not score. However, her senior year, the Olympic year of 1988, she not only qualified in the 200 individual medley but also finished third.

There are several reasons that all of this is significant to her authoring this book. Tracey was not at all competitive in butterfly, backstroke, or freestyle in her freshman year because of her technique, but through being a student of the sport and determination, she became accomplished enough in all the strokes to put together a great individual medley. Also, the faster she became at the individual medley, the faster she was in her "main stroke," the breast-stroke, thus surprising the nation at the 1988 Olympic Trials with two wins and an American record in the 100. Tracey McFarlane Mirande was an astute student of swimming as an athlete and remains so as a coach and teacher. I know that her knowledge will help you become a better swimmer and enjoy it more.

Every successful swimmer works hard, but I am convinced that what separates the great swimmers from the successful is technique. An athlete can spend only a certain amount of time in the water and can become only so strong or powerful. Eventually the great athlete understands the limitations of time and volume of training and begins to value technique efficiency as a major weapon in the training regime. Keep in mind that the faster an athlete travels through the water, the greater the resistance, and, therefore, the more important the elimination of resistance becomes; that is a huge part of technique. Also, the more efficient an athlete becomes in the water, the faster the athlete can travel without overtaxing his or her physiology, leaving more energy to finish the race well or to devote to the next segment of the triathlon.

I encourage young swimmers to use Tracey's book to work on all your strokes. Do not limit yourself to one stroke; the more you learn about all strokes, the more you will understand what makes your best stroke improve. And triathletes: work on backstroke as well as freestyle for muscle balance, improved kicking, and variety. The more you understand and develop backstroke, the more sensitive you will become to your freestyle weaknesses.

Enjoy this great book; use it to become a student of the great sport of swimming.

—Richard Quick
Coach, Stanford University and Team USA
Twelve-Time NCAA Champion Coach

ACKNOWLEDGMENTS

I would first like to thank my mother, Judy Mount, for giving me so many opportunities throughout my life and for spending hour after hour at various swimming pools across the country.

Thank you also to my two brothers, Michael and Dean McFarlane, for their love and support.

I would also like to thank the many talented swim coaches I have had during my swimming career, who taught me the finer details of the sport. Thank you especially to Richard Quick, who helped me develop into the swimmer I had always hoped to be.

Thank you to Rob Mirande for all of his help organizing the use of the pool at Trinity Prep School in Winter Park, Florida.

Thank you to my wonderful teammates at the University of Texas for your continued friendship and support.

Thanks to Todd Husty, our male swimmer for the photos, who swam at the University of California Santa Barbara and Trinity Prep High School and who is now a student at the University of Florida.

To Rowdy Gaines and Jenny Thompson, thanks for your kind words and support.

Last but not least, I would like to acknowledge the tremendous impact the sport of swimming has had on my life. It has provided me an education, opportunities to travel, and many lasting friendships, and for that I am forever grateful.

—Tracey McFarlane Mirande

There are many people who come together to take any book from concept to completion.

I would like to thank our editor, Mark Weinstein, of McGraw-Hill for his support. Mark was convinced that with the expertise of Olympic swimmer

Tracey McFarlane Mirande, this book would truly provide assistance to those who wanted to improve. Susan Moore—supervisor of editing, design, and production—handled the book production superbly under tight deadlines.

It's worth mentioning the challenges we had to overcome while preparing the manuscript for publication. We had to endure four hurricanes at the time we were concluding the writing of the manuscript and while we were attempting to schedule photography. Tracey was without power for a week after one storm and for a couple of days after the other. I evacuated twice and was, fortuitously, out of town for the other two. We considered ourselves lucky, though. When the day finally came to take the photos, there were torrential rains all around Orlando except where we were shooting. Todd Husty did a wonderful job for us swimming the butterfly and freestyle for the shoot. Tracey demonstrated the breaststroke and backstroke for the photos, and how much better can you get than having a former Olympian? Photographer Ben Van Horn stepped up with wonderful action shots.

For those who wonder whether the techniques described in this book work, I have to say without a doubt, yes they do. I met Tracey when I lived in the Palm Springs, California, area. I had already been a lap swimmer for 15 years but was never a competitive swimmer. And even though my daughter swam for 5 years, I didn't pick up much in the way of technique. I kept swimming the way I'd learned in lifesaving and water safety.

Tracey had come home to Palm Springs after she graduated from the University of Texas. While she fulfilled additional work to become a physical therapist, she coached the age-group team and a Masters team. I was one of the oldest and slowest swimmers in her Masters group. Most everyone else had been on a swim team or was a triathlete.

Probably because she couldn't stand looking at some of our stokes (including mine), Tracey taught us better technique, using the same drills that are in *Championship Swimming*. Not everyone needed it—there were some wonderful swimmers in the group—but I certainly did. It improved my strokes and taught me the value of a good coach. You can practice until you are blue, but if you are practicing the wrong things, you won't ever get better. Tracey's motto is "Practice doesn't make perfect. Perfect practice makes perfect." I still use the drills to reinforce the right form, and I am still trying to learn a decent butterfly.

And so, for giving me valuable assistance in improving my swimming, as well as for providing authoritative guidance and expert information for *Championship Swimming*, I'd like to thank Tracey. She's one of a kind and a true champion as an athlete and person.

—Kathlene Bissell

INTRODUCTION

If you have some basic swimming skills, *Championship Swimming* can help you learn to swim freestyle like a pro—and to look like one—in 30 days or less.

If you want to advance in swimming and learn backstroke, breaststroke, and even butterfly, *Championship Swimming* has all the inside coaching tips that will get you headed down the road to success with those strokes in another 21 days.

Whether you are a lap swimmer, triathlete, age-group swimmer, or just someone who wants to learn how to swim more proficiently, *Championship Swimming* will work for you. Whether you are 6 or 60, the only thing that matters is your desire to improve.

You do not have to be a good swimmer to use this book. The program in *Championship Swimming* is specifically designed for those who are not experts. You can be at the beginner level and use the program in this book to put your progress on the fast track. Olympic swimmer Tracey McFarlane Mirande has created simple step-by-step instructions, incorporating techniques that she has used with all levels of swimmers, from six- and seven-year-olds to Masters swimmers and triathletes as well as blue-ribbon-winning age-group swimmers. These step-by-step methods will work for you, too.

Championship Swimming is divided into three parts. Part I deals only with freestyle, because that is the stroke that most people want to swim. Part II is more advanced and includes backstroke, breaststroke, and butterfly. Part III has terminology, special swimming-specific exercises, and 12 workouts to keep you swimming long after you have completed every lesson.

In Part I, you will immediately start learning to swim freestyle, and by the end of the first week, you will have gone nearly a mile in the water. You will learn easy shortcuts to success, including how to put your body into the right position to swim efficiently and fluidly. You'll be surprised at how easy it is to swim when you learn proper form. Mirande also explains the whys behind techniques and the reasons certain methods work best.

In addition to technique instruction, each freestyle chapter has three workouts per week, because in order to get better at swimming, you have to swim. The workouts the first week are only 20 minutes long for beginning swimmers and include a separate workout for advanced swimmers. If you are a beginner, you will not be swimming the entire 20 minutes, because you will be taking rest breaks. Swimmers say that they swim only so they can have the rest breaks, and you will soon understand that you need to swim shorter distances now so you can improve and swim longer ones later.

The second week builds upon the freestyle basics learned earlier and concentrates on streamlining and improving your stroke.

In the third week, there is instruction for adding flip turns. Flip turns are not required for the program described in *Championship Swimming*, but if you are competing, you will want to learn them because they are faster than open turns.

By the end of the fourth week, you will be doing advanced swimming routines, including interval training. For those who are interested in speed, this chapter is devoted to learning how to swim faster.

Included in the chapter workouts are some additional challenge sets, and if you decide to do them, you will be nearing a mile per workout in the fourth week. (If you want to push yourself even further, there are additional workouts in Part III.)

Part II is for those who want to learn the other strokes: backstroke, breaststroke, and butterfly. While not everyone will want to learn the challenging butterfly stroke, many people like to swim backstroke and breaststroke. Different strokes use different muscles, and swimming these other strokes will give you an even more well-rounded workout. In addition, it gives you some variety in your workouts so that you aren't always doing the same thing.

The chapters in Part II are fast-tracked when compared with the freestyle lessons. One reason for that is because after learning freestyle, it will be easier for you to learn the other strokes, especially backstroke. In the backstroke chapter, there are three workouts that use both freestyle and backstroke, with extra focus on backstroke. In the breaststroke chapter, there are three workouts with freestyle, backstroke, and breaststroke, with extra emphasis on breaststroke. Similarly, in the butterfly chapter, there are three workouts with all strokes, including butterfly. Competitive swimmers may be most interested in butterfly and breaststroke because they are hard to learn, and there is a lot of misinformation when it comes to learning them.

Finally, Part III includes terms that you need to know in swimming, advice on how to find a swim team, exercises to strengthen swimming-specific muscles, and 12 weeks of workouts for two levels—beginning and experienced swimmers.

The methods in *Championship Swimming* work because we have seen the results—from helping age-group swimmers swim faster and better to helping triathletes become more successful. These techniques work in a hurry because swimmers using them have improved their swimming strokes in less than five minutes. So whether you are a future Olympian, a future Senior Olympian, or just a future great lap swimmer, *Championship Swimming* will work for you.

PART I

Chapter 1 covers all you need to know about pools, swimming gear, and safety. Chapters 2 through 5 get right down to the how-tos of swimming freestyle with proper technique. Freestyle is probably the most popular swimming stroke. However, many people who swim freestyle do not get the most out of their time in the water because they do not have efficient strokes. You can learn to swim freestyle like a pro by following the lessons and doing the workouts prescribed in each of the chapters that follow.

CHAPTER I

POOLS AND TOOLS OF THE TRADE

In reality, the only necessities for swimming are you and water that is deep enough so that your arms aren't touching the bottom. But for maximum enjoyment, you'll want to find a good swimming pool—and to outfit and prepare yourself appropriately. This chapter explains some of the fundamentals you will want to know when you are deciding where to spend your health club or pool dollars, as well as how best to ensure your comfort and safety when you're in the water.

SIZING UP A POOL

Lap swimmers define a *good* pool differently from "splashers"—the people who go to a pool to toss balls or play Marco Polo, tag, and the other pool games familiar to many of us from childhood.

The pool you select should be 25 yards long and several lanes wide. An Olympic pool—no matter what anybody's sales brochures tell you—is 50 meters long and usually eight lanes wide. The width of an Olympic-length pool in the United States is usually 25 yards. Internationally, pools are calibrated in meters. (A meter is 39.37 inches, or about 3⅓ inches longer than a yard.) You will rarely see a 25-meter pool unless you are swimming internationally.

In the United States, competitive swimmers train for two lengths of swimming: short course yards, which is done in a 25-yard pool, and long course, which is done in a 50-meter pool. Most competitive U.S. swimmers swim yards (short course) September through March and then meters (long course) April through August to allow them to prepare for international competitions and Olympic training, which is always done in meters. International swimmers will swim short course meters and long course. Competitive swim times are set for short course yards, short course meters, and long course. For example, my 100 breaststroke time is 1:00 short course yards, 1:07 short course meters, and 1:08 long course meters.

USA Swimming regulates the swim meets that are held in the United States. The length for competition in these events is in increments of 25 yards, and so most pools that hold meets of any kind are at least 25 yards.

That doesn't mean you can't get a good workout in a 20-yard pool, but when you get to the point where you can swim a half mile, you will probably want to look for a 25-yard pool so that you aren't spending so much time doing turns. You may not feel that the size difference is significant now, but as you get better, a short pool will annoy you.

A good pool will also have lane lines—those plastic ropelike dividers that mark off the lanes. Lane lines have several functions: they reduce waves, they organize a swim session, and they help to protect lap swimmers from less skilled swimmers and those who just plain aren't paying attention. By regulation, lane lines should change color 5 yards from the wall (5 meters internationally). This color change is a visual cue for swimmers that they are approaching the wall.

A deeper pool will be less wavy than a shallow pool. The ideal pool is 12 feet deep all the way across. However, most pools are 3 to 4 feet at one end and then have a diving well. In some facilities, you will find a deep lap pool and a separate diving well, but that configuration is an exception. Deeper water also equals faster speeds if you are racing because there is less turbulence. The deeper it is, the faster it is going to be.

Flow-through gutters also make a pool faster. With these structures, the water that splashes enters a drain in the gutter around the perimeter of the pool and flows back into the pool instead of crashing back onto the surface and causing more waves.

These features have a considerable impact on training and racing: if you train in a shallow pool with waves, it is going to feel different when you go to a race in a deep pool with less waves (and you'll probably make bigger improvements in your times). So be aware of this adjustment if you are competing.

Along with lane lines, I advocate that every pool have backstroke flags for swimmer safety. Backstroke flags, which all pools do not have but should, are triangular markers hung over the water at a distance of 5 yards from the wall, or 5 meters with 25- and 50-meter pools. The flags alert backstrokers that they are approaching the wall, to help them keep from hitting it with their hands or head.

Finally, the water temperature should be maintained within a specified range. Pools where competitive swimming is taking place shouldn't be heated to more than 82 degrees Fahrenheit. USA Swimming regulates the temperature for meets at between 78 and 82 degrees. A coach can stop a meet if the water is hotter. Remember, you'd likely be turning on the air-conditioning if your house was 78–82 degrees, so, really, it's a decent temperature. The state of Texas regulations for swimming pool temperatures suggest that 78–82 is ideal for swimming and cite negative side effects of hotter water, including increased evaporation and user discomfort—and, from an operating standpoint, increased scaling potential and increased use of disinfectants and fuel.

There is also a safety reason to be interested in water temperature. When you are swimming, you are exerting a tremendous amount of energy and generating a great deal of heat, and you are sweating. You need the water temperature to be in the proper range in order to stay cool. When the water is hotter than 82 degrees, it is hard for your body to cool off.

Some pools, unfortunately, keep the water hotter than that to satisfy the less active swimmers. So, before you join a club, ask: At what level do you keep your water temperature? If the pool gets hotter than the stated range, ask the staff to check it because, according to Dr. Joel M. Stager, director of the Counsilman Center, Department of Kinesiology, Indiana University, you can suffer heat exhaustion when your body can't get cool.

Nobody would do aerobics in a room that was 87 degrees. You shouldn't be swimming in hot water, either. In addition, hot water slows down swim times, so if you are training for a race, your training times will be much higher. You will feel tired sooner, as if you are slogging your way through a vat of pudding.

That said, a pool at 84 degrees is pleasant for most people, and unless you are a serious competitive swimmer, this temperature will be OK for you. Temperatures higher than that make your workout harder. And hot water— 88 degrees and above—can make it dangerous. Water at a temperature of 84 may feel a little cool when you get in, but after you have done a lap, it feels fine.

TRAINING EQUIPMENT

Like every other sport these days, swimming has training equipment to make you better and stronger and faster. Some of it works well, and some of it makes you worse.

If you are looking for swimming equipment, choose a sports store or a swim specialty store, such as Speedo, instead of the closest discount store. One popular company is Sports Authority, which carries many kinds of caps and goggles and also has some suits. There are several excellent online companies that used to be catalog stores before the birth of the Internet. For example, World Wide Aquatics, based in Cincinnati, has been around forever. The company is completely dependable for online or catalog ordering, and it has just about everything. See Chapter 9 for a list of other online and catalog stores.

Caps

Caps may be required at your pool. If you have long hair and intend to do lap swimming, you will want one to keep the hair out of your eyes and mouth. Also, a cap will protect your hair somewhat from pool chemicals. Nothing will protect your hair entirely, but a cap is your best defense. There are Lycra caps, latex caps, and silicone caps.

Lycra caps are beneficial in extremely hot conditions because they are fabric and so are better able to "breathe." However, they don't offer protection for your hair—though they do keep it out of your eyes. You can find one for between $10 and $15.

If you use a latex cap—which usually can be purchased for about $2—you will need to carry baby powder or cornstarch to shake in your cap after you are done swimming and have dried it. Dusting the cap with baby powder or cornstarch is the only way to keep it from sticking to itself after it comes into contact with the pool water. If you don't powder your latex cap, it will be a sticky mess, and you will be lucky if you can even separate it from itself. Baby powder or cornstarch can also be sprinkled on rubber goggle straps after a workout to keep them from deteriorating as quickly.

Silicone caps are a little more expensive, about $8 to $12, but they are easier to get on and off than latex. You aren't supposed to have to powder them when you are done, but it doesn't hurt them.

Goggles

At the very least, you will need goggles to protect your eyes from the pool chemicals, which make them burn. Goggles also enable you to see under water easily, and you will want to do that so that you can see where you are going and—for safety—see what is around you.

There are more kinds of goggles than Baskin-Robbins has ice cream. Goggles come with different colors of lenses and with a choice of plastic or foam padding—or without padding. I like foam ones, though with the foam-padded ones, you must rinse and dry them as you would your swimsuit to avoid "goggle rot." My coauthor likes the ones with no padding. Some people have gone to a mono-goggle because they say this style leaves less of a mark after swimming. Goggles are available from about $6 to $15 and can be as much as $30 to $40 for ones with prescription lenses.

You will have to replace goggles at least once a year because the pool chemicals eat the straps. Speedo does make a kit called Oggles, which is a new strap and nosepiece. However, the chemicals also eat away at the lens, making it hard to see out of, so if your goggles last you a year, you are doing well.

If you are swimming outdoors, you may want to consider goggles with dark smoke color lenses to lessen the brightness of the sun or reflective goggles, which are designed for the same purpose. Clear ones are suitable for indoor pools and for swimming at night. If you are nearsighted or farsighted, you can purchase prescription goggles. Some people—like me—wear their contact lenses when they swim. My coauthor, who is legally blind without glasses or contacts, doesn't. Keep in mind that the water will magnify, so, even if you are nearsighted, you will be able to see the pool bottom and side a little better with goggles than you can without your glasses.

Fins

People like to buy fins, but while I would definitely recommend fins for somebody who is just learning to do butterfly, I don't like them for freestyle or backstroke. Fins in freestyle and backstroke have a tendency to cause you to not move your feet, and they end up giving you too much knee bend in your kick. You can do drills such as the butterfly kick and breaststroke arms with them, but to swim laps with fins—no way. They will not be good for your stroke and will not make you better in the long run.

If you want to purchase them for butterfly, you can find a pair for $20 to $35. You do not need them for any other drills or strokes in *Championship Swimming*.

Pull Buoys

A pull buoy is used to isolate arm strokes. You put it between your legs, and it holds your legs up. I like the ones that are a solid piece of Styrofoam with a bigger end and a smaller end, but I don't know that any pull buoys are that much different from the others. Most are available for about $10.

Pull buoys can be an assist to swimming, but their main benefit is that they allow you to focus on your arms. You can get a little extra strengthening if you use a pull buoy in conjunction with paddles (see next section).

The advisability of using a pull buoy can depend on how good you are at floating to begin with. If your legs get tired when you swim, if you feel as if you are kicking hard and not getting anywhere, a pull buoy can help. For a beginner, it is a great aid because you are not fighting so hard to keep your legs up.

The downside of using a pull buoy is that it makes it difficult to roll from side to side, which you need to do in swimming, and so you have a tendency to stay flatter. Because the pull buoy is helping to hold your legs up, you can't roll as well. It is not a good idea to always use a pull buoy or to do your whole workout every day with one because it changes your stroke slightly, especially if it's the type that is bigger in back.

Paddles

Paddles are useful for strengthening the arms, shoulders, and pectoral muscles, which are heavily used in swimming. Paddles provide more resistance than your hands do, so the effect is like lifting weights in the water. Swimming requires many upper-body muscles that are not used in other sports, and that is one reason it is considered among the best exercises you can do for all-around conditioning. You use everything.

There are many kinds of paddles, and I am not a big fan of several of them, because most of them do not promote proper technique. I use Strokemaker, which is made by a company in Arizona. The paddle has an odd shape, more round than square. It is designed so that if you swim correctly, it stays on your hand. If you falter, it will come off. I like the Strokemaker because it has holes, and that allows you to have a bigger paddle; water can flow through it, but you still get resistance.

You can use Strokemaker paddles to swim any stroke, and they come in six sizes, 0 through 5—0 being the smallest and 5 the largest. Don't run out and buy the 5, though. With these paddles, most beginners should use a 1. When I was competing, I used a 2 or 3. Great male athletes use 4s and 5s.

You may use a different size depending on which stroke you are doing. I used size 2 for breaststroke and size 3 for backstroke and freestyle. No paddles for butterfly for me, although some very strong swimmers use them.

Strokemaker paddles are about $17 but worth it. Plus, unlike goggles, they last practically forever.

Kickboards

With a kickboard, you are higher in the water, not simulating proper mechanics. However, using a kickboard allows you to focus on your legs, and it strengthens the legs, which will make swimming freestyle easier in the long run. One thing kicking definitely does is use up oxygen; you can get winded from kicking because you're exerting the big muscles in your legs and glutes.

So, while I think there's a place for kickboards in a workout, in reality, if you train or work out properly, you are on your side for freestyle and backstroke. You should, theoretically, kick on your side for these two strokes. When you use a kickboard, however, you are flat in the water. But you are flat for breaststroke and butterfly, so using a kickboard for those is closer to actually swimming the stroke.

You have choices in the degree of flexibility among kickboards. I like the harder ones because they float better and are easier for beginning swimmers. Most are available for less than $15.

Watches and Clocks

In the ideal world, every pool would have a large pace clock on the wall so that when you work out, you can pace yourself and learn to do intervals. (Interval training is discussed at the end of this chapter and is the focus of Chapter 5.) If your pool doesn't have a pace clock, the best substitute is a triathlete watch—a waterproof watch that you can set to beep at specific times, allowing you to keep track of your interval times and rest times. We always say we swim only so that we get the rest break between the intervals. If you don't have a triathlete watch, you can make do with some other type of waterproof watch that has a second hand or a digital readout. If you are really dedicated, you can purchase a portable pace clock.

GETTING COMFORTABLE IN H₂O

Many people can swim but are still a little uncomfortable in the water. If you are tense and tight in the water, you probably have had a difficult time swimming. Being comfortable and relaxed in the water is a key to good swimming.

If you are completely at home in the water, skip right down to "Safety First." If, instead, you are one of those people who feel uncomfortable or a little nervous in the water, you need to convince yourself that—barring some extreme circumstance such as a meteor falling on you—you will stay afloat. One reason you will stay afloat is that your lungs contain air. Another is that your body contains fat. Even people with the lowest percentage of body fat still have some. And the more fat you have, the easier it is to float. That means many of us should have no problem at all!

Following are some tests you can do on your own to prove to yourself that you are more buoyant than you might think. While they may sound a little silly at first, they are designed to improve your comfort level and help you relax in the water. Remember, being relaxed will make you a better swimmer.

Penny Drill

To prove to yourself how hard it is for you to sink, drop 10 pennies on the bottom of the pool. It doesn't have to be deep—4 feet will do. Then, with your goggles on, try to stay down on the bottom while you pick all of them up. Or, if you don't have the pennies, just try to lie down on the bottom of the pool and stay there. You'll find that you have to fight to stay down. Your body wants to come up. If you try this a few times, you will convince yourself that, no matter how muscular you are, the tendency of your body is to rise to the surface, not sink to the bottom.

Floating Drill

Another experiment you can do to get more comfortable is to practice float-ing on your back. If you aren't supercomfortable floating on your back, try it first while you are holding on to the edge of the pool, to get the feel of it. It feels great. The water kind of gently pushes you up. It's the reason many people like to sleep on waterbeds. It's such a good feeling that it would be easy to nap right there in the pool.

But floating on your back has another purpose. As you progress in swim-ming, just remember, if you are out of breath at any time while you are in the water, you can always just roll onto your back, and there you are with plenty of air.

Now move away from the wall, out to where you have some room, and float on your back again. This time, stretch your arms out like a scarecrow. Take a deep breath, and you'll feel your feet, legs, and stomach rise. Blow the air out, and you'll feel your feet and legs drop a little. If you are very muscular, your feet may hang nearly straight down in the pool or fall so that your toes touch the bottom, but as soon as you take in a big breath, your chest will rise again because of the air inside your body.

Surface Dives

Go to about 8 feet of water and practice some surface dives. To do a surface dive, tread water, take a breath, and dive to the bottom of the pool; then push off the bottom with your feet and come back up. You will feel the pres-sure of the water as you go down, and you will feel yourself surge to the top coming up.

Somersault Drill

This drill gives you a sense of where your body is in the water and how to find the surface at any time. Standing in about 4 to 5 feet of water, do a som-ersault, landing on your feet and facing exactly the same way you started. If there are lines on the bottom of the pool, do this drill starting on a line, rolling over and ending up with your feet on the same line and facing the same direction. Be sure to blow the water out from your nose and mouth the entire time you are somersaulting.

You will need this skill to do flip turns later, so if you have never done a somersault in the water, go for it. It is easiest and fastest if you curl into a ball and then roll over in the water. Don't worry if you aren't perfect the first time. Most people mess it up the first six or seven times; they end up sideways or off center. Nobody gets it right the first time.

Once you are more at ease in the water, you will be more successful swimming, because you need to keep your body relaxed to swim like a pro.

If you need to practice the penny drill and floating drill a few more times before you get relaxed, do it.

SAFETY FIRST

A primary safety rule, applicable to even the best swimmers, is to swim with somebody whenever possible. If you can swim in a lifeguarded pool, it's always the smart thing to do. Many health club pools aren't lifeguarded, however. In those situations, you have to be your own lifeguard. While basic Red Cross water safety training says you shouldn't swim alone, many of us do it. Nevertheless, if you have a friend to work out with, so much the better and safer.

Equally important, don't swim if the water is too hot, if you are too tired, or if you have been drinking alcoholic beverages. And what about that old story about getting cramps from eating right before swimming? That's just what it is—a story. Some great swimmers eat before they swim; others can't swim on a full stomach.

While swimming alone is a no-no, the opposite extreme can also pose a problem. One person per lane is always the goal, but in busy places, sharing or circle swimming is the way to go. If the pool is crowded or there are people waiting, offer to share your lane and stay on your half. If you are sharing and everyone else is sharing and there are still people waiting, then it's time to circle swim. Proper circle swimming etiquette in a lap lane with three or more people is to stay on the right side of the lane going down, make a turn, and swim on the right side coming back. If there are a lot of people in the lane and they are faster than you are, stay on the right side and let people pass you in the middle of the lane or at the wall. In a large workout, there can be five, six, seven, or more swimmers in the lane at one time.

Check the rules of lap swimming at your facility to avoid accidents with other swimmers. If you are in a lane with an experienced swimmer, that is your best lane companion. The good swimmer knows where his or her body is in the water and will be watching out for you, too.

Even if you're following the lap swimming rules, there's still the possibility for injury. I don't know a lap swimmer who hasn't been hit with pool toys or had some non-lap-swimmer suddenly appear in the lane, causing a crash of heads or a whap to a body part. Usually that's a result of bad lifeguarding—or no lifeguarding—or of parents who aren't watching their children. It's annoying, and unfortunately pools can be dangerous, so you always need to be aware of what is going on around you in the pool.

Outdoor pools require special precautions. If your pool is outdoors and not lifeguarded, or if the lifeguards are off duty after a certain hour, be attuned to any approaching rain or thunderstorms. Here in Florida, thunderstorms can come out of nowhere, it seems. You can even get lightning with no rain and no actual visible storm system. The lightning rule is: If you see it, get out immediately. Wait until 30 minutes after the last lightning bolt before going back into the water. If you hear thunder, be on alert and start watching between laps for lightning. If there are other swimmers in the pool and they tell you they see lightning, get out. If you see it first, tell them to get out. It is ridiculously dangerous not to.

Indoor pools have different rules for swimming during stormy weather, and you should pay heed to what the lifeguards tell you in those instances. I have been in some indoor pools where swimmers were allowed to remain during thunderstorms and have been in others where we were asked to get out. Ask about the policy at your pool.

HYDRATING

Staying hydrated is a must for swimmers. I prefer water to sports drinks. If you choose a sports drink, dilute it 50 percent because of all the sugar and sodium. Those additives are dehydrating. If you dilute 50 percent, you will still get the flavor and electrolytes.

So, how much should you drink during a workout? How much to hydrate depends on how difficult your workout is. In a perfect world, we all would be drinking enough water so that we are hydrated when we get into the pool. If you are hydrated when you get in and you are swimming only a mile, you do not need to drink much water during the workout. On the other hand, if I'm an athlete swimming 7,000 yards, I should be drinking at least a liter during my workout. (Even older competitive swimmers are going 7,000 yards twice a day.) A swimming mile is usually considered 1,650 yards, though technically a mile is 1,760 yards; either way, a 7,000-yard workout is a considerably longer distance.

In summary, when it comes to hydrating, water is best, and you're better off having it handy when you don't need it than not having it when you do. Again, if you are swimming less than a mile and come to the pool hydrated, you are probably OK without a lot of water during your practice, but I would encourage drinking water immediately after your workout.

STRETCHING

It's a good idea to stretch before you do your workout. Swimmers need to stretch their rotator cuff muscles, triceps, hamstrings, and particularly pectoral or chest muscles. Here are several easy stretches that you should do before you swim. All stretches should be done for a slow count of 30 seconds and repeated three times.

- **Triceps stretch.** Raise one arm and bend it at the elbow so that your hand hangs behind your head. Place your other hand on your raised elbow and gently push it down and back, stretching the triceps. Switch arms and repeat.

Triceps stretch

- **Shoulder stretch.** This stretch is for your rotator cuff. Raise one arm and cross it in front of your body. Place your other hand on your elbow and gently pull it toward you.

Shoulder stretch

- **Pectoral stretch.** Position yourself in a doorway. With one hand on each wall at waist level, lean forward until you feel a stretch across the chest. Repeat twice, changing the position of your arms to shoulder height and overhead to feel a different stretch. This stretch can also be done with one arm at a time (see photo).

Pectoral stretch

IMPORTANCE OF RESTING

I encourage people who are just beginning their training to monitor how much rest they are taking. For example, if it's your first day and you are going to try to do 500 yards—a fourth of a mile—you may be able to do only two lengths at a time. Maybe you can do just one. Given that you're just starting out, you might have to take a long break to recover—as much as several minutes. Keep track of that, and try to decrease the amount of rest you take each time. If there is a pace clock at the pool, or if you have a waterproof watch, you can use it to help you chart your swimming time as well as your resting time. If you want, you can write down your time after you finish, but most people just remember it by watching the pace clock.

In this example, if you are doing two lengths (50 yards total) at a time, ten times, for a total of 500 yards, that is referred to as "ten 50s."

We call swimming a certain length on a certain amount of rest interval training. We swim a certain distance and rest a specified length of time.

Usually, for lengths of 50 or 100 yards, we have no more than 15 to 20 seconds of rest. We call that "doing 50s on 15 rest" or "doing 100s on 20 rest." Sometimes, with a long swim, such as 500 yards, you might rest 30 seconds or even a minute.

To improve, if you have been doing ten 50s (50 yards ten times), the next time, do the same overall yardage, but try to do 75s with the same rest break. Continue to increase your distance until you are able to do 200 yards without a break. Swimming 200 yards without resting should be the goal for beginners.

Once you are in good swimming shape, you are going to pay close attention to the amount of time you spend swimming versus the time resting. As an example, true sprinters (those who swim 50 yards or meters in swimming meets) might train with a 3:1 ratio, meaning that they rest three times as long as they swim. In most workouts, however, the average swimmers will rest very little relative to the amount of time spent swimming. Distance swimmers may swim up to a mile at one time, rest 20 seconds, and swim another mile at the same speed. Every workout should have varying distances and rest breaks to train all muscle fibers and all energy systems—aerobic and anaerobic.

Now that we have the basics out of the way, let's get in the water and have some fun.

CHAPTER 2

FREESTYLE BASICS

Week 1: 20 minutes each session; three sessions

For this lesson, you will need:
Goggles and cap
Kickboard (optional; many pools have kickboards you can use)
Empty 16-, 20-, or 24-ounce plastic water bottle with cap on

To help you learn the right way to do freestyle, I will explain the strokes and illustrate them with pictures. If you have a buddy who can help be your eyes to make sure you are doing what you should be doing—conforming with the pictures—you will know that you have it. If you don't, that's OK. The stroke drills will get your body into the right position to become a better swimmer, to swim like a pro. If you do the drills, your body will tend to go into the right position automatically, which is why the drills are important.

Even if you are an experienced swimmer, if you want to be better and faster, remember: practice doesn't make perfect; perfect practice makes perfect. Practicing the wrong action over and over doesn't improve your stroke or your speed. Practicing the right technique will.

Practice new technique for short distances at first, even if you are experienced. When we get tired, which we all do after we swim distances, we tend to revert to old habits. We lose our stroke. We lose our form. We lose proper technique. The best way to learn the right technique is to start with shorter distances until the new technique is ingrained. Then gradually add distance. The idea is to learn to hold your stroke for whatever distance you are swimming. If you are a triathlete and are doing the Ironman, you may have to learn to hold your stroke for up to 2 miles. So, for you, learning to hold the proper technique is also extremely important. It will take a lot of effort and training to hold your stroke that long.

Swimming is different from weight training: with swimming, the more you do it, the better you get. A minimum of three times a week is recommended, which is why I have included three workouts per week. If I take more than a day off, I notice a difference. However, it's nice to have a day's break to recover. The amount you swim depends on how good you want to be. Competitive swimmers swim five or six days a week, and older (12 and up) age-group swimmers will occasionally increase to two-a-days (two separate workouts in one day) in the summer. In college and training for the Olympics, we swam 6,000 to 9,000 yards per workout, nine times per week.

However, for most people starting out in lap swimming, 20 to 30 minutes per session is fine. If you are beginning, you may do only 400 or 500 yards in this time. If you are advanced, you can go to the longer workouts.

Keep in mind that the 20–30 minutes isn't constant swimming. That would be difficult to impossible for somebody starting out. When swimmers train, we take breaks. We seldom swim more than 400 or 500 yards at a time unless we are training for distances of 800 or 1,500 yards. We usually do a combination of shorter distances: 50s, 100s, 200s. So, think of this as 20 to 30 minutes with many rest breaks. You need to rest, especially when you are starting.

Even if you are experienced, you are trying to learn new technique, and so it is a good idea to rest often because your body will be performing in different ways from what it was used to.

FLOAT FIRST

Your first exercise is floating on your stomach. Float and look down at the bottom of the pool; try to have your legs up near the surface, with the back of your heels just out of the water. Think about where your legs and feet are.

Floating is important because with freestyle, you want to make sure your head is relaxed and your legs are close to the surface of the water without having to try. If you can do this, you are in great position to begin freestyle basics.

If you have a hard time floating, put your arms out to the side, as if you are trying to fly. If you are very muscular, you will have a harder time floating, but it's not impossible.

STREAMLINING

In any swimming stroke, you want to be as streamlined and efficient as possible. Streamlined = efficient = faster. You want to reduce the resistance your body has as it travels through the water. To test this for yourself, push the water with your palm. You can feel the resistance of the water against your hand. (It's also a great way to make a good splash at somebody.) When you are swimming, you want to reduce that resistance, and so instead of pushing your palm against the water, you want to go fingers-pointing-first through the water.

Try it. Push your hand straight out in front of you, thumb up and fingers first. It glides right through with much less resistance than your palm. That is the basic concept of streamlining. Reducing resistance by putting your body in the right position is the essence of learning to swim well and to have it look effortless. It is never effortless, by the way, but some people sure look great when they swim, and you can too.

When you swim, you will almost never actually be flat on your stomach for freestyle. Your time is spent mostly on your side. An Olympic swimmer doing freestyle is never flat in the water. The hips and shoulders rotate together. No matter what it looks like on TV, a freestyle swimmer is not flat.

In freestyle, it's not enough to just reach with your arms; you have to roll your hips and shoulders. The only time you are on your stomach is when you are going from one side to the other. You will be on your stomach for butterfly or breaststroke, but never for freestyle.

In freestyle, you rotate from side to side with your whole body as you pull yourself through the water in a streamlined fashion, almost as if you have a

When you swim, you will almost never actually be flat on your stomach. Your time is spent on your side. Here you see the swimmer's back as he reaches with his right arm under the water.

metal pole all the way through your body like a shish kebab. You rotate around it.

Many people swim as if they are snowplows. Their shoulders act like the snowplow blade pushing the water out of the way as they move their arms. This is similar to your palm pushing across the water. It's not streamlined. It's harder to do. It's not efficient, and if you have done this in the past, this chapter will show you how to stop doing that and start swimming with ease.

When you are streamlined, you can get 6 inches more reach than you can get when you are plowing. You want to be as tall and skinny as you can be, reaching as far and long as you can. That's the image you have to have in your mind when you swim. Reach as far as you can with each stroke.

KICKING MECHANICS

Even if you have done lap swimming in the past, you must train your body to get into the right position. In fact, if you have already been swimming and doing it the wrong way, this is even more essential, because you have to relearn what to do and correct years of bad habits. I am going to start you on the way with a kickboard and kicking. But first, let's review kicking fundamentals so that you're practicing the right way.

Your kick should be with a mostly straight but relaxed leg, kicking from the hip, not bending at the knee. The bending should be at the ankle, with the foot moving back and forth, toes pointed but relaxed. Move your legs from the hip and make small, baby kicks, so that your feet are *no more than 12 inches apart* at the widest. You want enough space between your feet during the kick so that you are moving some water.

Kick with your legs nearly straight, your toes pointed, and your feet getting no more than 12 inches apart at the deepest part of the kick.

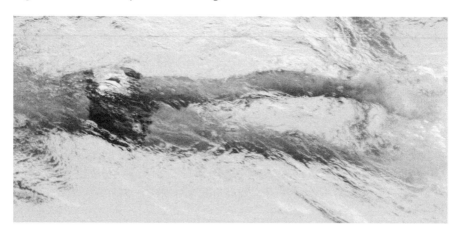

You will have a problem if you are too tense. So, try to make it a relaxed move from the hip. You will waste energy if you are tense. Loose, relaxed legs—but with toes pointed—is the rule. Let your ankles be loose.

Strive to avoid the common mistakes that people make in swimming or in practicing kicking. One is surface kicking, in which the only thing being kicked is air. The feet are too high. This gets you nowhere.

Another is kicking too deep. The legs are too far apart with each kick, which wastes energy.

A third is having too much knee bend, using only half of the leg instead of using the power of the whole leg. This is a common mistake that runners and bikers make when they go to the pool to try to learn swimming for triathlons.

KICKING DRILLS

You can do these drills without a kickboard, but you'll have an easier time with a kickboard, especially if you can't already swim a half mile.

Lie on your side in the water, holding on to the kickboard with one hand. Stretch out as long as you can, and kick all the way down the pool.

If you can't make it through a whole lap kicking, go as far as you can. Try for at least halfway. Don't worry about speed. It doesn't have to be fast. It needs to be right. Just keep kicking. Try to relax your head and arms, as if you are lying on the sofa, with the water as your pillow.

When you get all the way to the end, you may need to rest and catch your breath. If so, do it. We will get to proper rest interval times later, but for now, if you are winded, rest. If not, immediately turn onto your other side

To practice the correct kick, lie on your side with a kickboard and kick the length of the pool.

and kick back. If you made it only halfway and need to rest, rest. Then turn onto your other side and return to your starting point, kicking on that side. Rest again. Now you know what kicking on your side feels like. (For the experienced swimmer: yes, this drill is also for you. The only difference is that you can probably do the 50 yards without resting, and you can do it faster.)

Next is the "10/10" drill with kickboard. Take the kickboard again. Lie on your side. This time, after every 10 kicks, switch sides, kicking down the pool to the other end and returning.

So, if you start on your left side, you will be lying on your left side, holding the kickboard in your left hand and with your left arm outstretched completely; your face will be out of the water enough so that you will not have a problem breathing. To switch, move your right hand up from wherever it was in the water and grab the kickboard with it; immediately let go of the kickboard with your left hand and roll over to your right side, all the while kicking. Count 10 kicks, and then change back to the side on which you started. Continue for two pool lengths.

It doesn't matter whether you start with your right or left. If you can't make it 25 yards, stop in the middle and rest but continue the remainder of the way until you have gone two pool lengths—up and back.

If you have done four pool lengths at this point, you have gone 100 yards.

BOTTLE DRILLS

Instead of using the kickboard, you will now use your empty water bottle. Make sure the cap is screwed on well so that no water gets in.

Lie on your side again, this time holding the bottle in your hand, and extend your arm while kicking. It's important to keep your arms extended in this drill. Kick 10 times on one side, and then switch hands and rotate by putting your face in the water and rolling to the other side. Kick 10 times on that side with your arm extended, and then switch hands again, putting your face in the water as you rotate to the other side, kicking all the while.

This is what you do with your breathing: Take a breath before your face goes into the water and blow out all the air under water; when you roll to the other side, you will be ready to take a breath. Repeat that all the way down the pool. Do this for the entire pool length, if you can make it, or until you need to rest and catch your breath.

Lie on your side, holding an empty water bottle, with your arm extended in front of you. Kick 10 times, and then roll to the other side by switching hands on the bottle.

If you have made it the full pool length, rest at the end, if you need to, and come back. If you have not made it the entire pool length, rest, floating on your back, until you can make it the remainder of the way. Do two full pool lengths, even if you have to rest in midlap. Then repeat this whole exercise, going all the way down the pool and all the way back.

You have now done 200 yards, or about an eighth of a mile.

Next, do the same drill but switch sides every six kicks. Do two entire pool lengths. By now, you are approximating the same kind of move that you will make when you swim properly.

You have done 250 yards.

At this point, if you feel that you need to repeat any drill to become more comfortable doing it, repeat it. If you feel that you have it mastered, then go on to the next step. But do not skip a step. And never be reluctant to come back to these basic drills to work on your stroke mechanics. Remember, practice doesn't make perfect; perfect practice makes perfect.

BREATHING "EVERY THREE"

Now you are going to add the arm stroke and breathing and actually start to swim. When you swim freestyle, you should breathe every three arm strokes—or "every three." That means you will breathe on both sides of your body, right and left. Don't say you can't. You can! This section will explain and show you how.

From a physical therapy point of view as well as from a coaching point of view, I find that people who do not breathe every three will roll well to one side and not well to the other. They end up leaning on one arm or making an unusual move with one arm, causing an uneven stroke. They develop shoulder and neck problems. The longer you go breathing to one side, the harder it will be to make the change, and the worse your mechanics will get.

If you breathe every three, you have a tendency to have a balanced stroke. Even if you start out swimming more slowly while breathing every three, it is better in the long run. And it will be faster in the long run. It is harder to do if you are used to breathing every two strokes. If you are just starting out, it is a great habit to get into. If you have been swimming a long time and have not tried it, just remember that it will allow you to reach farther with that other side, and you will soon go faster.

If you are a triathlete, do this retraining when you are not getting ready for an important race. It takes a while to learn to breathe every three if you have been breathing every two.

Since you have just done breathing from both sides with the bottle drill, you already know what it feels like.

BREATHING MECHANICS

To breathe, you have to learn to blow air out. Blow it out your nose and mouth. If you could, you would want to blow it out your ears, but we aren't wired that way. You will remember to breathe in, but you must teach yourself to blow air out; that is the only way your lungs will be ready to take in more air.

Breathing properly is easy. All you do is follow your hand as it goes under water and turn your head to the side. As you perform your arm stroke, your hand will pass under your face. When that happens, begin to turn your head to that side, just enough to take in air, and then put your face back in the water as your hand passes your face out of the water.

When you breathe, you should be looking to the side of the pool but slightly behind you.

When you swim, take three arm strokes, and in the third arm stroke, turn your head to the other side to take a breath.

A common mistake with breathing is raising the head instead of turning it to the side. If you think of the cartoon character Popeye, it is easier. Pop-

When you swim, take three arm strokes, and in the third arm stroke, turn your head to the other side to take a breath.

eye has one open eye and talks out of one side of his mouth. That's what you want to do when you breathe. You want one eye and one side of your mouth out of the water and the other eye still in the water. Another way to think of it is to keep one goggle under the surface for freestyle breathing. Just turn your head to the side when you see your hand; keep one goggle in, and turn so that one goggle is out. Try it once or twice just leaning over in the water, and you will see how easy it is.

The reason you don't want to raise your head is that as soon as you do that, your hips and legs drop in the water and create drag, slowing you down and making it much harder for you to swim. Turning your head to the side helps you swim faster and more easily.

Now we will go on to the arm stroke for freestyle.

FREESTYLE ARM STROKE MECHANICS

In freestyle, your hands should enter the water fingertips first, middle finger first, so that your elbow is high and bent when your hand meets the water. Think of it as slipping your hand into a long sleeve.

You want your hand in line with your shoulder, about 12 inches out in front of you if you are an adult. Slide your fingertips in, and then move your hand forward all the way into the water. Extend your arm as far as you can as you rotate onto your side, like you did in the bottle drills. This cuts down on drag—or resistance.

When you have extended your arm as far as you can, cup the water slightly with your hand. It feels like a lump of wet sand. With your hand, first sweep out slightly, no more than 6 inches wider than your shoulders, and catch the water. Then sweep back in, making almost a half-hourglass shape, with the narrow part being underneath you, level with your waist. Pull the water past you.

To understand how it should feel, think of playing tug-of-war and pulling on a rope one hand at a time or of climbing a ladder one rung at a time. It feels like that, but with the motion sweeping slightly out and then slightly back in.

Pull your arm all the way down until it is past your waist and extended and your hand is by your thigh. That's when you are done with your arm stroke.

A common mistake people make with their arm stroke is putting their hand flat on the water instead of entering fingers first. If you put your hand

In freestyle, your hands should enter the water fingertips first, middle finger first, so that your elbow is high and bent when your hand meets the water. Slide your fingertips in, and then move your hand forward all the way into the water. Extend your arm as far as you can as you rotate onto your side.

Pull all the way down until your arm is past your waist and extended and your hand is by your thigh.

out flat onto the water, you will catch too much air and go more slowly because you aren't moving as much water. Entering the water with your hand at a slight downward angle will begin a long, powerful stroke, which is what you want. Again, you want to be as long and tall and skinny as you can be, rolling onto your side and reaching as far and long as you can. Your goal is to move as much water as you can with each stroke, and to do that, you need to reach as far as you can.

Another common mistake is not reaching far enough. Some people put their arm in the water just a couple of inches beyond their head. That is not nearly long enough to give you the kind of power you want.

A third common mistake, and this one is particularly easy to make if you are breathing every two instead of every three, is crossing over the centerline of your body when your hand enters the water.

Crossing over the centerline of your body with your arm stroke, above or below the water, is an error to avoid.

A common mistake is taking the hand out of the water before the stroke is finished.

Some people even put a hand in so that it is practically over the opposite ear. If you have had this problem in the past, breathing every three and learning to extend will really improve your swimming ability in a hurry.

Yet another common mistake is not finishing the stroke. Some swimmers don't pull water all the way until their hand is next to their thigh. They take it out of the water too soon. A later drill will help you avoid that.

And finally, there is the mistake of not bending the elbow. Some people fling their arm out as if they are doing the butterfly. This wastes energy and is dangerous to others in the same lap lane.

Your elbow needs to bend instead of being straight.

Remember that the shortest distance between two points is a straight line. Imagine drawing a straight line from your thigh to where your hand should enter the water. For your hand to get from your thigh to the water, the elbow must bend. We will have a drill for that later, too.

Recapping: Slip your hand, fingers first, into the water. Extend your arm as far as you can and then sweep out, catching the water with your hand, and sweep in, pulling the water underneath you and past you until your arm is extended in back and your hand is near your thigh, palm toward the sky. It may help you to practice this technique in front of a mirror before heading for the pool.

BOTTLE DRILL WITHOUT THE BOTTLE

Next you will do the bottle drill, kicking 10 times on each side, but without the bottle. You will add an arm stroke.

Lie on your left side, with your left arm extended, and kick 10 times. Then roll to the other side, just as you did in the bottle drill, but this time, pull under the water with your left arm while you reach over and into the water with your right arm. Extend your right arm as far as you can, and lie on your right side and kick 10 times. Remember to blow air out as you put your face in the water and take air in when your face comes to the surface. Do an entire pool length of this. Then rest. Then do another pool length and rest.

This can be a difficult drill even for those who have done a lot of lap swimming. But stay with it. Remember, you get to rest at the other end.

If you are an experienced swimmer, you may not need to rest, but you still need to do this drill. In fact, this drill is extremely important for you because it gets you into the correct position to do freestyle. So, the stranger this feels, the more important it is for you to do it. If you are experienced, you should do four 25s or two 50s of this drill. If you have been breathing every two and are an experienced swimmer, you should definitely do this drill.

Now do the drill changing sides every 6 kicks instead of every 10. Rest and swim back, doing the same thing. If you are experienced, do four lengths or two 50s, switching every 6 kicks.

At this point, you are practically swimming, but the difference is that you are breathing every time you roll to the side.

Now you will start real swimming. And to do that, we are going to change the emphasis from using your kick as your guide to using your arms.

FREESTYLE STROKE MECHANICS

Instead of rolling to the side every six kicks, you will roll to the side with every arm stroke. But you will keep your face directed at the bottom of the pool except for every third arm stroke, and that's where you will breathe. Every three arm strokes, you will breathe by rolling to the side. Say to yourself: It's one, two, breathe on three; one, two, breathe on three.

Remember, on the strokes where you aren't taking a breath, look down at the bottom of the pool. It has a dark line on it. Just look at that. Looking down at the bottom will help you keep your legs up. And if your legs are up, that will make it easier to swim. So, unless you have already been a competitive swimmer, try to look down at the bottom of the pool—that way, your legs are sure to be closer to the surface.

Don't worry about counting the number of kicks at this point. One of the most famous distance swimmers in U.S. history, Shirley Babashoff, used a two-beat kick, one kick for every arm stroke. She held distance freestyle records until Janet Evans came along.

If you can coordinate your kicks at this point, great. If not, concentrate mostly on the arms and breathing. Kicking keeps your legs up and reduces drag, making it easier for you to swim and easier for you to swim faster. That's part of the purpose of the kick. It might be two kicks per arm stroke (or "per arm"), or one, or three. Do whatever works for you.

Kicking hard at this point in your progression will take too much energy, so you have to balance it out. Distance swimmers use a two-beat kick, one for every arm. Distance swimmers trying to do 200s use a four-beat kick, two for every arm. Real sprinters use a six-beat kick, three for every arm. I have had only one student use a six-beat kick in workouts, because the quads—those big muscles in your leg—fatigue. They are the biggest muscles in the body. People can't maintain that pace through a long, hard workout.

What you are doing now—working on coordinating arms and breathing—is the hardest part of learning to swim properly. It's not important to do it fast. In fact, at this stage, slower is better. It's important to do it right and learn the rhythm.

FINAL DRILL

So, to start, push off the wall while lying on one side to give yourself some momentum.

Take a breath and then make your arm strokes. Breathe in when you are rolling to the side every three strokes. Breathe out when your face turns and goes under the water and you're looking at the bottom of the pool. It will be one, two, breathe on three; one, two, breathe on three; one, two, breathe on three; one, two, breathe on three—all the way down the pool. Breathe = your third arm stroke. That rhythm will help you get it right at first. If you are already a fast swimmer, you may want to say: one, two, breathe; one, two, breathe.

When you get to the end of the pool, stop and rest. If you are experienced and can keep up the breathing pattern, do 50 yards instead of 25. Those who are new to this should do five more lengths. If you can go more, great. But you can stop your first lesson now.

Experienced swimmers should do five more 50s, breathing every three. You can stop here or add this to one of the workouts at the end of the book.

You have just done the hardest part—well, except for butterfly—and you are on your way.

WORKOUT 1

Remember to rest when you become winded. If you are new to this, try to keep rests to less than 30 seconds. If you're experienced, rest 15–20 seconds. Distances of the workout lessons are in cumulative yards: (400) = 400 yards. (International swimmers should just use the same number for meters—i.e., 400 meters instead of 400 yards.) *Instructions and yardage totals for experienced swimmers are in italics for all workouts.*

1. All levels: Float and look down at the bottom of the pool. Let your legs come up. Get accustomed to what that feels like. Your heels should be near the surface.

2. All levels: Do one 25, kickboard or kicking without board, lying on your side. Rest. (25)

3. All levels: Do one 25, kickboard or kicking without board, lying on your side. Rest. (50)

4. All levels: Do two 25s, kickboard or kicking without board, on your side, rolling and switching sides every 10 kicks (10/10 drill with kickboard). Rest at each end if needed. (100)

5. All levels: Do four 25s, kicking holding a bottle (10/10 drill with bottle). Rest at each end if needed. (200)

6. All levels: Do two 25s, kicking holding a bottle, six kicks each side and then switching. Rest at each end if needed. (250)

7. All levels: Do two 25s 10/10 drill, rolling to other side every 10 kicks. (300)

8. Do two 25s 6/6 drill, rolling to other side every six kicks. (350) *Do four 25s 6/6 drill, rolling to other side every six kicks. (400)*

9. Swim 25 yards, breathing every three arm strokes. Rest and repeat. (400) *Swim 50 yards. Rest. (450)*

10. Repeat 25-yard swim four more times. (500) *Swim six more 50s, resting 15–20 seconds between each. If you want more work, check the workouts in Chapter 11. (750)*

WORKOUT 2

1. All levels: Do two 25s, kickboard or kicking without board, on your side. Rest at each end if needed. (50)

2. All levels: Do two 25s, kickboard or kicking without board, on your side, rolling and switching sides every 10 kicks (10/10 drill with kickboard). Rest at each end if needed. (100)

3. Do two 25s, kicking holding a bottle, six kicks each side and then switching. Rest at each end if needed. (150) *Do two 50s, kicking holding a bottle, six kicks each side. Rest 15–20 seconds between each. (200)*

4. Swim four 25s 10/10 drill. Rest at each end if needed. (250) *Swim four 50s 10/10 drill. Rest 15–20 seconds between each. (400)*

5. Swim six 25s freestyle, breathing every three arm strokes. (400) *Swim six 50s, breathing every three. Rest 15–20 seconds between each. (700)*

WORKOUT 3

1. All levels: Do two 25s, kickboard or kicking without board, on your side, easy kicks, concentrating on having a relaxed but mostly straight leg. Rest. (50)

2. Swim two 25s 10/10 drill. Rest after each. (100) *Swim two 50s 10/10 drill. Rest 15–20 seconds after each. (150)*

3. Swim 25 yards 10/10 drill. Rest. Swim next 25 freestyle, breathing every three arm strokes. Rest. Repeat three more times. (300) *Swim four 50s as 25 yards 10/10 drill and 25 yards free, breathing every three. Rest 15–20 seconds between each 50. (350)*

4. All levels: Do two 25s, kicking freestyle with kickboard or lying on your side. (350) *(400)*

5. Swim two 25s freestyle, breathing every three. Rest after each. Then swim one 25 10/10 drill and rest. Repeat. (500) *Swim two 50s freestyle, breathing every three. Then swim one 50 10/10 drill. Rest 15–20 seconds between each. Repeat. (700)*

6. Swim 25 yards easy freestyle, breathing every three arm strokes. Rest and repeat. (550) *Swim four easy 25s. Rest 15–20 seconds between each. (800)*

CHAPTER 3

FREESTYLE STREAMLINING AND LAPS

Week 2: 30 minutes each session; three sessions

For this lesson, you will need:
Goggles and cap
Kickboard (optional)

This week, we will add some new concepts and skills to your repertoire: more streamlining techniques including pushing off properly, drills to reinforce the proper stroke, plus workouts designed to help you progress.

In addition, no matter what you were doing last week, this week you should *breathe every three arm strokes every time* you do a regular swimming lap. It is important to get into this habit, and the only way to do that is to do it.

PERFECT PRACTICE MAKES PERFECT

The workouts for this week do not have long distances because you will need to practice the breathing until you are comfortable enough with it to swim 200 yards while breathing every three. That may take a while, and the time it takes depends on what swimming condition you are in now. Even an experienced swimmer will have a hard time swimming 200 yards breathing every three if he or she has been breathing every two.

Part of the reason breathing every three is harder is obvious: if you have been breathing every two strokes, you have to go one more stroke before you get air. Combining breathing every three *and* extending your stroke as you learned to do with the 10/10 drill means that you are also pulling approximately 6 inches more water with each stroke. That's an additional 18 inches of water—a half yard—with every breath. So, if it feels harder to do both of these at once, it's not your imagination. It is harder. That is one reason that both the workout sets and the lengths you swim have been short.

Another factor contributing to difficulty in breathing only every three strokes is muscle fatigue. One thing I tell people who are contemplating a long workout while they make a change in stroke is to think about how many strokes they have to take. Your body is able to do only a certain number of strokes before the muscles fatigue. That's speaking from a physical therapy point of view. You are able to put your arm over your head and use those muscles only so many times before fatigue sets in. After fatigue sets in, you are going to make some compensations. You will start making errors. That is also another reason I have given you shorter distances in the workouts, even though you may be used to swimming longer ones: I want to reduce or eliminate errors.

If you are an experienced swimmer, you will want to make these kinds of changes at the beginning of your season—when you are a little out of shape and when you wouldn't be swimming as much in a daily workout. Likewise, if you are a triathlete, you will want to make the changes several months before an important competition. You do not want to make them a week before a big meet or event. On the other hand, if you are a year-round lap swimmer who does not compete, you can make the changes at any time.

No matter which category applies to you, it's going to take a while before you can build up to your earlier yardage. Just start with 500- to 700-yard workouts, practicing properly to build good stroke habits. Then increase your yardage. You can probably increase the yardage by 100 yards per workout without a problem.

You are already up to at least 400 yards. If you hope to take that to 4,300 yards tomorrow with an improved stroke, you'll discover that it is just not going to happen. It will take several weeks of building up and getting stronger, as well as training your muscles to move in the right way.

Swimmers sometimes complain about "losing" their stroke when they're tired. When fatigue sets in, instead of your hand going purposefully into the water fingers first, you might slap at the water palm first. Instead of reaching as far as you can, you are likely to shorten your stroke because it gets too hard to keep reaching out. Instead of rolling from side to side, you might get flat again. Your elbows could get too low. You might not finish every stroke. Any number of bad things can happen when you get tired. Errors such as those are what is meant by losing your stroke.

No matter how skilled we are, when our muscles get tired, we start to make mistakes. *If you keep swimming while you are making mistakes, then you are practicing an error.* That's yet another reason I have kept the swims short in the beginning. I want you to practice and learn the right thing, not the wrong thing. I know it's hard to be patient, but if you want to get better, this is what you need to do, and this is the way you need to do it.

If you want to do longer workouts and believe you can hold your stroke throughout, then just go to Chapter 11, select part of a sample workout, and add it to the workouts I've given you. But don't skip these shorter workouts and drills. If you skip them, you won't build the base of fundamentals that you need for success. Always remember: practice doesn't make perfect; perfect practice makes perfect. I would rather see you spend two or three weeks swimming shorter distances to build solid fundamentals than see you groove an error.

After three weeks or so of breathing every three strokes, if you try to go back to breathing every two strokes, it will feel wrong. Breathing every three will feel right. After three weeks of reaching out on every stroke and rotating from one side to the other in your stroke, swimming flat will feel wrong. You won't want to go back to the earlier way, because you will have made the improvement. You won't ever have to go back.

It's tough to unlearn bad habits, but the sooner you learn the right strokes, the sooner you will be a better, faster swimmer.

Now we're about ready for this week's important new step: pushing off the wall and streamlining as you start every lap. Before that, though, you need to know a little more about what streamlining is and why it is important.

STREAMLINING TO REDUCE DRAG

Everything we do in swimming is designed to make our bodies move in a more streamlined fashion so that we have less resistance to the water. The less resistance—or drag—we have and the stronger we are, the faster we can swim.

In competition, reducing drag is taken so seriously that both male and female swimmers shave their bodies to reduce the drag of body hair. There are swimsuits designed to have less water resistance than skin. Every hundredth of a second counts in competition because often that is all that separates first place from second and third. We do everything we can to make ourselves as efficient and sleek in the water as possible.

All the new things we did last week aid in streamlining. The way your hand goes into the water fingers first aids in streamlining. The way your body rotates as you swim freestyle aids in streamlining. The 10/10 drill that we did last week, and will do again this week, helps get your body into a position to be more streamlined. It makes your shape more like the bow of a ship and less like a tanker or a snowplow.

Just getting into the right position will make you faster than you were before, but it takes a few weeks to learn a new position so that it's ingrained. It also takes a little while to get strong enough to pull that extra 6 inches of water in each stroke when you swim in a fully streamlined position. In fact, if you were to do nothing else correctly but streamlining, rotating, and reaching, you would become faster after growing accustomed to pulling the additional water. And that's my goal: to make you a faster, more efficient swimmer.

Now let's get to the mechanics for pushing off from the wall.

STREAMLINED PUSH-OFF

Pushing off from the wall the right way is how you get streamlined from the start. This week, pushing off will become part of what you do from now on. Every 25 or 50 or 75 or 100 that you do will start with a new, streamlined push-off from the wall. If you are not doing flip turns, you will use this streamlined position every time you turn. Even if you are doing flip turns, you still need to push off from the wall in a streamlined position after your turn. Learning flip turns will come later, and you may never want to learn them, but we will cover them in the next chapter for those who do want to know how.

Competitive swimmers spend countless hours practicing starts and turns because that can make the difference in winning and losing a race. So, whether you are just trying to improve for your own fitness goals or are racing in age-group or Masters swimming or in sprint triathlons in which pools are used for the swim, having a streamlined turn can make a big difference in your results. If you are an age-group or Masters swimmer, it can make the difference in whether you win or lose a race. (See Chapter 9 for information on joining a team for age-group or Masters swimmers.)

Using a streamlined push-off can also make swimming easier, because you shorten the distance that you actually have to swim. With a 5-yard push-off at each end, you are swimming only 20 yards each lap instead of 25. Combining that with your improved, streamlined body position sliding through the water will make you faster, because a good swimmer will make it 8 or 9 yards before taking the first breath.

Instead of pushing off from a position in which you are standing in the water or holding your hands in front of you and making a minidive into the water, you will begin each lap with a streamlined push-off.

STREAMLINED PUSH-OFF START MECHANICS

Pick the side on which you want to lie for every start, your right or your left. For convenience and convention in circle swimming, it makes sense to pick the left side as the one that enters the water first for your push-off, but you can use the right side if that is more comfortable. I lie on my left side, as does my coauthor, but that doesn't mean that you have to if lying on your right feels better. No matter which side you pick, here is what you do:

1. Hold on to the edge of the pool with one hand. This would be the right hand if you are going to lie on your left side, and vice versa.

2. Turn so the side of your body is facing the wall, and get submerged up to your neck and ready to lie on your side just below the surface of the water.

3. Put both feet up on the wall, with your knees bent at a 90-degree angle, so that you are ready to push off.

4. Point the hand not holding the wall toward the opposite end of the pool, with the arm extended, just as you did in the 10/10 drill.

5. Drop down under the water about 12 inches, push off with your legs, and glide on your side. Dropping down puts you under the surface instead of on top of the water where you have more drag.

6. As you push off, reach into the water with the hand that was on the edge and extend both of your arms over your head and lock your hands together with your thumbs. Your arms should be tight to your ears, with one hand flat on top of the other.

7. As you glide under the water, kick at least six times with a small, quick kick and angle up to the surface.

8. Without taking a breath, make your first two arm strokes, and then breathe on your third stroke.

9. You should be at least 5 yards from the wall before you take your first stroke. You will know it's 5 yards because at that point, the lane lines should change color or go from solid to alternating colors.

That is a streamlined push-off. It gets you started faster every time for freestyle. If you are using open turns instead of flip turns, making a stream-

The streamlined push-off. Hold on to the edge of the pool with one hand and get submerged up to your neck. Extend your other arm and get ready to lie on your side. Put your feet on the wall with legs bent, ready to push off. Let go of the wall, drop down under the water, push off with your legs, and glide on your side. As you push off, extend both arms overhead and lock your hands together. As you glide under the water, kick at least six times with small, quick kicks as you angle up to the surface.

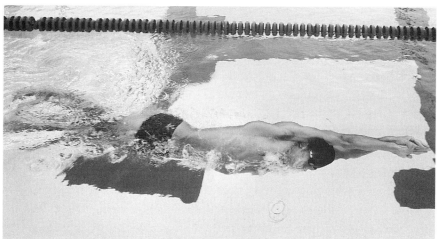

lined push-off from the wall will take several seconds off your time for 100s. By the same token, if you are swimming in Masters or doing a half-mile pool swim in sprint triathlons, this will help you drop your times significantly, unless you have been doing flip turns already.

Practice making a streamlined push-off from the wall with kicks. Do six push-offs. Try to go at least 5 yards with your push-off and then start stroking. If you need to practice 10 times, do it. You should not be starting your stroke until you get to the 5-yard mark—the point where the color markings on the lane lines change.

Now start your first lap, pushing off from the wall using a streamlined start with kicking, and then do the 10/10 drill for 25 yards. As you will see, making a streamlined push-off from the wall gets you into exactly the position in which you need to be to start the drill and also to start your stroke. When you get to the other end, if you need to rest, do that. If not, continue by first pushing off in a streamlined position, but this time, swim 25 yards breathing every three instead of doing the 10/10 drill. Repeat.

Next, push off, including the small kicks, and swim 25 yards and rest; then do the same thing to come back. Experienced swimmers should do 50 yards, pushing off, gliding, and kicking at the turn just as you do at the start. If you are doing flip turns, be sure to add the streamlined position and the kicking to them if you have not been doing that.

From now on, every time you leave the wall for freestyle, push off in a streamlined position and kick-start your lap. This is forever. Put it into the mental file for what you do every time you leave the wall for freestyle.

Now we are going to add some new drills—one for each of the following three workouts—to help reinforce streamlining in your arm stroke.

FINGERTIP DRAG DRILL

The first drill is the fingertip drag drill. To do this drill, you swim freestyle, breathing every three arm strokes, but as you bring your hand up from your thigh area to above your head where it enters the water, you will drag the surface of the water with your fingertips. Drag your fingertips the whole distance from your hip area to entry, and then enter the water fingertips first. Your elbow will bend and be higher than everything else, pointing to the sky.

The fingertip drag drill is designed to help you get your hand from the finish of one stroke to the start of the next stroke the shortest way possible. That makes your stroke more efficient and makes you faster. It also helps

The fingertip drag drill
helps you get your hand
from the finish of one
stroke to the start of the
next stroke in the
shortest way possible. It
also helps you get used
to bending your elbow.

you get used to bending your elbow in the stroke, which will allow you to get your hand from your hip to the entry point faster. In addition, it helps you enter the water fingers first instead of palm first.

Don't try to rush the fingertip drag drill. Feel where your arm is and where your elbow is when you do this drill. It may feel funny at first, but this drill will help your hand draw a straight line between your hip and the entry point for the next stroke. You will probably find the fingertip drag drill easier to do the first time than the 10/10 drill.

Do four 25s of the fingertip drag drill, pushing off the wall in a streamlined position each time, or two 50s if you are experienced.

WORKOUT 1

At the end of each workout is a challenge set. It is optional but will help increase the intensity of the workout as well as the yardage. *Instructions for experienced swimmers are in italics for all workouts.*

1. All levels: Push off streamlined with kicks. Do this 5 to 10 times, until you can do it every time with ease.

2. Push off streamlined with kicks, and do 10/10 drill for a 25; rest if needed; then push off streamlined with kicks, and swim 25 breathing every three. Repeat. (100) *Push off streamlined with kicks, and swim 50, using push-off and streamlined turn and breathing every three. Repeat. (100)*

3. All levels: Push off streamlined with kicks, and swim either four 25s or two 50s breathing every three. (200) *(200)*

4. All levels: Fingertip drill—four 25s or two 50s, streamlining off the wall and kicking. (300) *(300)*

5. Swim four 25s, concentrating on having a good stroke, streamlining off the wall and kicking; rest no more than 20 seconds if possible—30 seconds if you must; then try to swim one 50, streamlining off the wall at both ends. (450) *Swim six 50s, concentrating on having a good stroke, streamlining off the wall and kicking at starts and turns or doing flip turns with kicking off the wall. Rest no more than 15–20 seconds between each. (600)*

6. All levels: Do four 25s as 25 yards 10/10 drill, 25 yards fingertip drag drill, 25 yards 10/10 drill, and 25 yards fingertip drag drill. (550) *(700) Challenge set (optional): Do two 75s, streamlining off the wall and kicking at starts and turns or doing flip turns with kicking off the wall. (850)*

FLICKING DRILL

For workout 2 this week, I am adding another drill to your practice session. It is the flicking drill. Its purpose is to make sure you finish every arm stroke.

To do this drill, as you finish each arm stroke, instead of lifting your arm out of the water, flick the water up into the air with your hand and then reach for the next stroke. This is not an easy drill to do at first. You will use

In the flicking drill, you push the water up at the end of each stroke.

your triceps muscles in this drill. As you will discover, the triceps are extremely important in swimming. In fact, if you weren't sure where your triceps are, you will be after you do this drill.

WORKOUT 2

1. All levels: Push off streamlined with kicks. Repeat 6 to 10 times.

2. Do 25 yards 10/10 drill and 25 yards freestyle; rest 30 seconds. Repeat. (100) *Do two 50s as 25 yards 10/10 drill and 25 yards freestyle. Rest 20 seconds maximum between each 50. (100)*

3. Do two times: 25 yards fingertip drag drill, 25 yards regular freestyle. Rest 20 or 30 seconds between each 25 if needed. (200) *Do two 50s as 25 yards fingertip drag drill and 25 yards regular freestyle. Rest 20 seconds between each 50. (200)*

4. Do two times: 25 yards flicking drill. Rest after each. (250) *Do four 25s or two 50s flicking drill. Rest after each. (300)*

5. Do two 25s freestyle and one 50 freestyle, resting 20 seconds maximum, if possible, between each. (350) *Do four 50s freestyle. Rest 20 seconds between each. (500)*

6. Do 25 yards 10/10 drill; 25 yards fingertip drag drill; rest; 25 yards flicking drill; 25 yards freestyle; rest. (450) *Do 25 yards 10/10 drill, 25 yards fingertip drag drill, 25 yards flicking drill, and 25 yards freestyle as 100 yards. Rest 30 seconds and repeat. (700)*

7. Do two 25s and one 50 freestyle using a good stroke. Rest as needed, but try for 20 seconds maximum between each. (550) *Do three 50s and one 100 freestyle. Rest 20 seconds between each. (950)*

COMBINATION DRILL

For workout 3, I am adding a drill that combines the fingertip drag with the flicking drill. In this drill, for every arm stroke, as you take your arm out of the water, you first flick the water up in the air, and then you drag your fingertips all the way to the point where your hand enters the water. It is easier to get the rhythm of this drill if you do three regular strokes and then start adding the fingertip drag and the flicking combination.

Remember, every lap is breathing every three, and every turn has a streamlined push-off with kicking.

WORKOUT 3

This workout combines everything you have learned up to now and adds an extra twist or two. Also, to get you ready for next week—when I will start teaching you how to do a workout so that you are conditioning yourself for improvement—this workout has more emphasis on swimming and less on drills. I am sure you are happy to hear that. However, these drills never get old. They are always good to use in workouts to remind your muscles what you should be doing—especially the 10/10 drill, which really gets you into the right position for good swimming.

You will start this session by warming up, and you will end it by cooling down. Even though it's not a long distance today, starting every session by warming up your muscles and ending by cooling down helps prevent injury. If you start swimming fast right from the beginning, you are liable to injure a muscle. And if you don't cool down, you are liable to get stiff because the lactic acid doesn't have a chance to work out of your muscles.

Warming up should be done slowly. Think of yourself almost as swimming at half speed at the start. This gets your muscles moving, gets your lungs used to breathing, and gets oxygen flowing to all the parts of your body that will need it. Swimmers who are accustomed to swimming a long distance may want to double the warm-up. When you are swimming longer workouts, 2,000 to 3,000 yards and more, you will probably want to take as much as 400 yards for warm-up.

1. Warm up: Swim two 25s slowly and easily. Reach and extend each stroke, making yourself as long as you can. (50) *Experienced swimmers can do two 50s but must do at least two 25s. (100)*

2. All levels: Kick two 25s with a kickboard or lying on your side in the water. If you're on your side, change sides after first 25. (100) *(150)*

3. All levels: Swim, with a good stroke, 25, 50, 25, 50. Rest 20–30 seconds at each stopping point. *Better swimmers should rest 15–20 seconds.* Try

to keep the rest periods the same even if you feel that you are slowing down when swimming. (250) *(300)*

4. All levels: Do 50 yards 10/10 drill. Rest at 25 if needed. (300) *(350)*

5. Do 25 yards combination drill—flicking and fingertip drag—and then swim 25, resting 20–30 seconds, as follows: 25 drill; rest; 25 freestyle; rest. Repeat three times. (450) *Combination drill and swim 50 yards as 25 drill and 25 swim. Repeat three times. Rest 20 seconds between each 50. (500)*

6. Swim two 25s, two 50s, two 25s, resting 20–30 seconds after each. (650) *Swim two 50s, two 75s, one 100, resting 15–20 seconds after each. (850)*

7. Cool down—swim slowly, as though you are going in slow motion. Do two 25s. (700) *Cool down—do two 50s. (950)*

CHAPTER 4

WORKOUTS TO IMPROVE DISTANCE AND CONDITIONING

Week 3: 30–45 minutes each session; three sessions

For this lesson, you will need:
Goggles and cap
Pace clock or stopwatch or triathlete's watch

Congratulations. You have made it to week 3. This week, the workouts begin to get more rigorous. If you are experienced, you are probably saying that it's about time. But if you are newer, what you already have been asked to do is a lot to learn in a short time. If you feel that you need to repeat week 2, go ahead. Most people who could swim 25 yards before starting this program will be fine with the progression. But if you are one who could go only half a pool length before, you might want to repeat week 2 before going on. Read through this lesson, and then make your decision.

This week, we will start to work on learning how to practice the right way to improve your conditioning. Getting into the right conditioning for swimming will help you swim faster, just as using the combination of proper mechanics will. This chapter also introduces you to the right way to practice to improve your speed.

REDUCING REST TIMES

Many swimmers go to the pool with a goal of swimming 20 minutes because they are told that's the ideal length of time for aerobic exercise. They wonder why they don't get faster or better. The reason is that they are not working on improving their swimming conditioning. To improve swimming conditioning and eventually speed, you need to be able to reduce the amount of rest you take between laps. In the second workout this week, I will ask you to do that.

If you have been taking 30 seconds between swims of 25 yards, try to reduce that to 25 seconds. If you have been taking 20 seconds, try to reduce it to 15.

When I tell you to swim two 25s with 25 seconds of rest, that means you rest 25 seconds after your first 25 and then immediately start your second 25, even if you are slightly out of breath. If I tell you to swim two 50s with 15 seconds of rest, you should rest for only 15 seconds after swimming 50 yards and then start the second 50 yards, even if you are slightly out of breath. This is the only way to improve your speed and conditioning. We will do it gradually, and you will probably be able to do it the first time, since this is your third week.

Some weekend triathletes who were not competitive swimmers start swimming just to get to the length they need for a competition. Then they swim that, or half of that twice, in a workout, particularly the sprint triathlon distance, which is 800 yards. Constant swimming of a certain distance or for a certain time alone will not necessarily improve swimming speed; you will maintain what you are able to do, but you will not necessarily improve. You need to push yourself to improve.

So, if you have been wondering why you are not going faster, the reason is probably that your practice sessions have not been designed to give you the right kind of conditioning challenge to help you get faster. In Chapter 5, on learning speed, I will teach you much more about it.

Also this week, in addition to reinforcing what you have already learned, I will help you get used to the kinds of practice you will do if you decide to advance in swimming. Whether you want to join a Masters group or just beat the person in the next lane at the health club pool, these workouts will give you a taste of what you might do later. Remember, too, that you can always advance without joining a team. There are many places to purchase workouts, and some websites will send you workouts for free. Some people, though, just like the misery-loves-company factor of being in the pool with other swimmers, or they need to be with a group to be motivated.

Let's get started. Beginning now and continuing forever:

1. You will stretch before every workout.
2. Every time I ask you to swim a certain distance, it needs to be with a streamlined push-off and kicking off the wall.
3. For freestyle, you will breathe every three strokes, unless there is a special drill to do something else.
4. You will do streamlined push-offs or streamlined flip turns with kicking after the turn.

I won't repeat those instructions anymore. If you have done the first six workout sessions, you should have the instructions ingrained by now. If not, by the end of this week, you probably will.

LEARNING HOW TO WARM UP

As I said in the last chapter, before any long or hard workout, you need to warm up the muscles in your body. Now that you know you can swim, you need to add this step to your workout every time. In warm-up, you never want to swim your fastest; you want to swim at a moderate speed.

You will also want to learn to cool down, or "warm down," after a workout. That is also done at a moderate speed. The warm-down helps eliminate muscle soreness from lactic acid buildup. Think of yourself as a Thoroughbred racehorse. Before a race, it warms up, and after a race, it warms down.

If you get to the point where you are swimming longer workouts—2,000 to 3,000 yards—you should try to do at least 400 yards of warm-up. Some people who are especially muscular may need more warm-up. You will get to know what your body needs, but whatever the case, don't skip this step. If you get to longer workouts, you will also want to add 150 to 200 yards of warm-down.

Because these early workouts are relatively short, the warm-ups and warm-downs are also short. They are included to help you learn to how to do them and to get you into the habit.

In our first workout for this week, here is what your warm-up will be:

- Newer swimmers, swim four 25s freestyle, resting 20–30 seconds after each 25, easy to moderate speed. (100 yards)
- Experienced swimmers, swim four 50s, resting 15–20 seconds after each 50, easy to moderate speed. (200 yards)

Then, the first thing I want you to do after warming up is to experiment. You will need a pace clock or a watch to do this drill properly, so be sure to have one.

COUNTING STROKES AND TIME

No matter what your experience level, do three 25s, counting the number of strokes you take and the amount of time you need to swim 25 yards. Swim it at a speed that is comfortable but not loafing and not all-out fast. The number of strokes will probably be about the same or slightly higher for the third 25-yard swim. Remember the average number. Example: If you needed 29 strokes the first time, 30 the second, and 31 the third, your average is 30 stokes. Do the same with the times. If it's 40 seconds, 42 seconds, and 44 seconds, your average time is 42.

Now swim another 25 and try to reduce the average number of arm strokes by 1. The only way to reduce the number of arm strokes is to really reach out with each one. You will find it hard to do.

Now try another experiment. If you needed 30 arm strokes and took 40 seconds to swim 25 yards, swim another 25 and try to reduce the total number—30 + 40 = 70—by 1. Either use 1 fewer arm stroke or swim 1 second faster—your choice. You will find that doing either is difficult—but it's a great way to extend yourself in practice.

If you were successful, try to reduce the total by 1 more. If you weren't successful, try it again. (250 yards) *(350 yards)*

This activity is important because, ideally in a workout, you want to swim with the fewest number of strokes necessary and still maintain speed while reaching out to take that extra 6 inches of distance in each stroke. What's the right number of strokes per 25 yards? A world-class male swimmer will take 8 strokes per lap. A world-class female swimmer, 10 strokes per lap. You might take anywhere between 20 and 40.

Don't get discouraged if you take 30 or even 40. Remember that a world-class male gets 8 to 10 yards off the wall with his flip turn before he takes his first stroke. A female gets about 8 yards before she takes a stroke. That means the men are really swimming only 15 to 17 yards per 25-yard length. The women are swimming about 17 yards per 25-yard length. They also cut down another yard going into their flip turns.

Just to keep myself honest, I tried counting my strokes in a practice swim a few days ago. Given that I haven't been training for the last 10 to 12 years, I took 15 arm strokes per lap. I probably took 12 or 13 when I was in training. My specialty, however, was breaststroke, not freestyle. Nevertheless, when you swim workouts at world-class level, you are expected to be reasonably good at all the strokes, not just your specialty.

However, the reason for the experiment—adding your strokes plus your time and then subtracting 1—is that the more streamlined and extended you are, the fewer strokes you have to take to reach the other end of the pool. The fewer strokes you take, the less fatigued your body will be. That's why trying to get to the end of the pool with 1 fewer stroke or in 1 less second is a valuable exercise.

INCREASING DISTANCE

With this week's workouts, I will also increase your distance slightly. And I will also add some challenge sets for those who feel they can do a little more. Don't feel that you have to do them. Do them if you can or if you want to.

This week, you will also do some different distances. If you have been doing 25s, it's time to try 50 yards with the same rest as when you did the 25s. If you have been doing 50s, it's time to try some 75s with the same rest break. That's how you get into swimming condition. You want to increase your yardage with the same or less rest time. That is how you know you are improving. The long-term goal should be to swim 200 yards and then to swim a second 200 yards with only 20 seconds of rest between the two and not have your time suffer a lot from the first 200 to the second 200.

You still need to be focused on having a good, long, streamlined stroke, no matter what the distance. But, as you will see, it gets a little more difficult to keep swimming at the same pace with a long stroke as the distance increases. That is why you have to make the increases gradually, not all at once.

In last week's lessons, I said that you would not be able to go from 400 yards to 4,300 yards overnight or in a week, but you can certainly get to that distance with consistent work. If you have been doing long workouts in the past, you can get back to that distance by gradually working up to it, adding 100 yards a session, which would be 300 yards a week if you swim three workouts a week. That way, you will be certain to keep your new, improved stroke and add to the length of your workout.

Even if you have been swimming just 25 yards at a time, within a few weeks you should be able swim 100 yards at a time, depending on your conditioning level. When you reach that point, you will want to work until you can do 200s with 15 or 20 seconds of rest. You won't do that now, but in

Chapter 11 there is a progression of workouts that will get you up to that 200-yard level and beyond. Once you see what it takes to get to 200 yards, you will have even more appreciation for expert swimmers who may do a set of 800-700-600-500-400 with 20 seconds or less of rest between each distance.

Now, if you don't believe you can do it, let me tell you about a swimmer named Nick. He started swimming when he was 65 because his doctor told him that his health was so bad that he should put his affairs in order and—if he wanted to stay alive—start an exercise program. At this writing, he is 82 and can swim a one-hour session. He was not a swimmer before. So, there is pretty much no excuse for anyone's saying it's too hard.

WORKOUT 1

In the first session this week, newer swimmers have a workout that is 475 yards or 675 yards. Experienced swimmers have a workout that is 625 or 925 yards. If the longer length is too much for you now, just do the shorter distance. *Instructions for experienced swimmers are in italics for all workouts.*

1. Warm up—swim four 25s freestyle, resting 20–30 seconds, easy to moderate speed. (100) *Warm up—swim four 50s, resting 15 seconds, easy to moderate speed. (200)*

2. All levels: Swim three 25s, counting the number of strokes and the number of seconds you take to do each length; rest 20–30 seconds between each 25. Calculate the averages. (175) *(275)*

3. All levels: Add average time and average number of strokes together. Swim one 25 and try to reduce your total by 1—either 1 fewer stroke or 1 second faster. Repeat. (225) *(325)*

4. If you have been swimming 25s: Swim one 50; rest 20–30 seconds; swim two 25s; rest 20–30 seconds. Repeat. (425) *If you have been swimming 50s: Swim one 75; rest 15–20 seconds; swim one 50; rest 15–20 seconds. Repeat. (575)*

5. Challenge set: Swim two 25s, resting 20–30 seconds between each; swim one 50; rest 30 seconds. Repeat. (625) *Swim 25, 50, and 75 with 15–20*

seconds of rest. Then reverse it and swim 75, 50, and 25 with 20 seconds of rest. Don't stop between the increase and the decrease. *(875)*

6. All levels: Warm down—swim two 25s easy. (475) (675) *(625) (925)*

WORKOUT 2

For this workout, you will try to reduce the amount of rest between laps. It may seem a little bit hard the first time. Your goal should be to reduce your rest time by 5 seconds. If you have been resting 30 seconds, try to rest for 25 or 20 seconds. If you have been resting 20 seconds, try to rest for 15. If you have been resting 15 seconds, try to do 10. If you are not able to reduce the amount of rest time this week, try again next week. When you are able to reduce your rest time even from 30 seconds to 25, you are starting to get into swimming condition. You should see this as real progress, because it truly is.

1. Warm up—swim four 25s freestyle, resting 25 seconds, easy to moderate speed. (100) *Warm up—swim four 50s freestyle, resting 15 seconds, easy to moderate speed. (200)*

2. All levels: Do 25 yards 10/10 drill and swim 25—try to swim it as 50 yards if you have not done this before. Rest 30 seconds if you're newer, 15 seconds if you're experienced. Repeat. (200) *(300)*

3. Swim two 25s, resting 20–25 seconds between each. Rest 30 seconds. Repeat. (300) *Swim two 50s and one 25, resting 10–15 seconds between each. Rest 20 seconds. Repeat. (550)*

4. Swim two 50s with 30 seconds of rest, and then immediately two 25s with 25 seconds of rest. Rest 30 seconds after the second 25. Repeat the set. (600) *Swim 25, 50, and 75 with 15 seconds of rest. Rest 20–30 seconds after the 75 if needed—15 is ideal. Repeat. (850)*

5. Challenge set: Swim 25, 50, and 75 with 25–30 seconds of rest. (750) *Swim two 75s with 15 seconds of rest, immediately followed by one 50. (1,050)*

6. Warm down—swim two 25s easy. (650) (800) *Warm down—swim two 50s easy. (950) (1,150)*

LEARNING FLIP TURNS

For the last session in week 3, I will explain flip turns. I will give you six easy steps, with plenty of directions and photos.

To do flip turns safely, you need to be in a pool that has marking lines on the bottom of each lane and a cross symbol (+) on the wall at the end of the pool. If your pool does not have the cross symbol on the wall, it may not be safe for doing flip turns. You need some kind of a visual mark or tile design to guide you in making the turn, and you need a T mark on the bottom of the pool to know when to make your flip.

If you are working on speed, you absolutely need to learn flip turns. If you are not working on speed, learning flip turns will improve your swimming conditioning and will enable you to flow more fluidly when you are swimming longer distances.

The flip turn is also used for backstroke, which is explained in a later chapter, so it is important to get it right for freestyle so that you'll have it for backstroke.

If you are already doing some kind of flip turn, you may want to review this portion just to make sure that your mechanics are on target. Errors are common. In addition, the flip turn has changed somewhat over the years. This chapter provides the latest, most efficient method.

Learning the flip turn will also help you look like a pro in the pool, even if you never get to competition speeds.

One warning: Be sure to stretch your hamstrings before trying flip turns. If you know that you are typically tight in the hamstrings and you are practicing turns at the end of your workout, you may want to do a hamstring stretch before trying them.

The way to put flip turns into your workout is just to make a commitment to do a flip turn at every wall every time you do 50 or more yards. That way, you will eventually figure out where you need to start your turn. No matter how awkward it feels, no matter whether it's a good one or an imperfect one, do it at every turn. Make that commitment, and soon you will be flipping with relative ease at every turn.

It does take more effort to do flip turns in a workout. So, the first time you do one in a 50-yard swim, you will probably feel as if you have gone longer than 50 yards before you finish. This is normal. Like everything else, doing flip turns takes some getting used to.

My coauthor used to do workouts of three 600-yard sets—one freestyle, one backstroke, and one breaststroke. When she wanted to add flip turns, she just added them to the freestyle. If she missed a turn, she went back and did it and then kept going.

Some swimmers learned a half-twist kind of a flip turn, which used to be taught years ago, but that is not the kind of turn that is taught today. The new method is faster, so if you are in Masters competition, you will want to make the change.

Now I'll explain what you need to do to learn how to do flip turns. You may want to practice all of this at the end of the second session for this week or before you begin the third workout. Or you may want to split it up and do a couple of steps in the second session and the remainder in the third one. It depends on your level of determination.

How to Do Flip Turns

What I will have you do before you try to do a flip turn at the wall is to practice plenty of them without being near the wall. That way, you get the feel of what to do without the pressure of worrying about the wall.

The T at the end of the lane on the bottom of the pool is the guide as to when to do a flip turn. The goal is to flip and then park your feet on the cross on the wall at the end of the pool for a millisecond, and then push off.

When I do a flip turn, this is my sequence:

1. I take one arm stroke after the T at the bottom of the pool, and then both arms are at my sides.
2. Before I flip, with my arms at my sides, I'm staring at the wall, still kicking.
3. I flip and immediately turn my palms up and pull the water up toward my head, doing a biceps curl underwater while I flip. That extra underwater pull with the arms helps me flip faster.
4. I hit the cross on the wall with my feet, landing with them shoulder-width apart and my knees bent about 90 degrees. I am getting ready to jump off the wall.
5. As soon as I jump or push off the wall, I twist onto my side and extend my arms up over my head and lock my thumbs, which puts me into a position that is identical to the streamlined push-off we practiced earlier.
6. I kick five or six times and take one arm stroke, and then, in the second arm stroke, I take a breath and begin swimming the next lap.

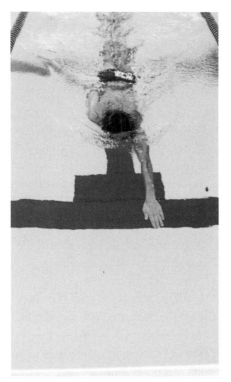

Take one arm stroke after the T on the bottom of the pool, and then your arms will be at your sides. Continue kicking and then flip over. Put your feet on the cross on the wall and push off on your back. As soon as you push off, turn on your side, kick, and prepare to start the next lap.

It sounds a lot more complicated than it is. I will teach you in six simple steps, and you will be able to learn it easily.

Step 1: Beginners Pre-Flip-Turn Mechanics

1. The first thing you must do is learn to blow water out of your nose and mouth for about 6 seconds. This will keep water from getting in your nose. Practice by going under the water and blowing out in a slow-release fashion. Count as you blow out: one thousand, two thousand, three thousand, four thousand, five thousand, six thousand, and then come up for air.

2. The next skill you will need is to be able to turn a somersault in the water. Try that, blowing air out of your nose and mouth the whole time. Be sure to blow air out of your nose and mouth during the entire turn to keep from getting water in your nose when you flip over. If you are not experienced at doing somersaults in the water, you may feel disoriented or

dizzy at first. But if you try a few more, you will get your bearings. Here's a tip: The tighter you curl, the faster you turn. And the faster you turn, the less disoriented you will be.

3. Stand on one of the lines on the bottom of the pool. Do a somersault, and end up with your feet on the line and facing the same way as when you started.

4. Do several somersaults like that. If you use your arms, you will turn faster. When I'm teaching children, I ask them to see how many somersaults they can do before taking a breath. Usually they can do five or six with one breath. If you want to try that, go for it.

Step 2: Flipping Out

Now I want you to do what we will call the flipping-out drill. Swim 25 yards, and after every three arm strokes, do a somersault flip in the middle of the pool and then keep on swimming. So, it's three strokes and flip, three strokes and flip, three strokes and flip. If you have to do four or five strokes between flips, that's OK.

The purpose of this drill is to get you comfortable with the somersault motion and with swimming into a somersault, because that is what you will do with a real flip turn. Try another 25 yards of that.

Step 3: The Wall

This step is the front half of the flip turn. You know how to flip. Now you are ready to add the wall. All you do in this step is flip over and park your feet on the wall, toes pointing up.

To start, stand in the water at the flags or where the lane lines change color, about 5 yards out from the wall.

Swim toward the wall, and when your head crosses the T at the bottom of the pool, take one more arm stroke and, just as you did in the flipping-out drill, flip over with your arms at your side, pull your arms up toward your face in a biceps curl, and place your feet on the cross on the wall. Then stop. You should be about 12 inches below the surface of the water. Your toes should be pointed up, 12 inches below the surface.

Most people miss the wall, coming up short, the first time—even the first four or five times. It is only natural, because you are propelling yourself toward the wall, and it takes a little courage to do it.

If you can't reach the wall on your flip by taking one arm stroke after the T, then try it with two arm strokes. You will probably not need three. Be sure to use your arms and the biceps curl underwater to help you flip over faster and propel you toward the wall.

The second most common mistake is to try to twist while you are flipping. Almost everybody does that the first time. Many people get into some other discombobulated, pretzel-like position. Some people end up completely sideways. Don't worry about it. Almost nobody does it right the first or second or even third time. After 5 to 10 times, you will probably get the hang of it. Once you have it, you have it. If it takes 20 times, it takes 20 times. No matter: when you get it, you get it. This is the hardest part. The rest is really easy.

Some people have a hard time convincing themselves that there is room for them to fit and flip. But unless you are 6′6″ and swimming in a pool that is less than 3 feet deep, you will probably be fine. Sometimes young kids are told to swim until they touch the wall with their fingertips and then curl up into a ball and put their feet on the wall and push off the wall. While it's not the way I would teach you to learn the flip turn, it is a handy way to convince yourself that there is plenty of room between the T and the wall for just about anybody to make a flip turn. My coauthor can do this, and she is 5′7″.

Step 4: The Push-Off

Next we will add the push-off. Start 5 yards out, swim and do a flip, land your feet on the cross, about 12 inches below the water, and extend your arms over your head in a streamlined position and push off on your back, angling up to the surface. Repeat until you get this step. You should end floating on your back, looking up.

The most important thing to remember is that you never leave the wall on your stomach. This is another common mistake. You don't get anyplace near being on your stomach until you are rotating after taking your first stroke following the turn. As you know by now, you are hardly ever on your stomach in freestyle. You also do not want to turn over onto your stomach in your flip turn.

Step 5: The Push-Off plus Twist

Now do a flip, land your feet on the cross, about 12 inches below the surface, and, as you extend your arms over your head in a streamlined position, push off and twist onto your side—just as you would in a streamlined push-off from the wall—and angle up toward the surface and kick. Repeat until you get this step.

Common mistakes at this stage include coming off the wall too shallow or too deep. Everybody messes that up once or twice, too. Do a few more until you get the angle right so that you come up to the surface at about the 5-yard mark. Your end point may be shorter than that, or it may be longer, depending on how strong your push is.

Step 6: The Flip Turn, Push-Off plus Twist, plus Swimming

Now do a flip, land your feet on the cross, about 12 inches below the surface, extend your arms over your head in a streamlined position, and push off and twist onto your side—just as you would in a streamlined push-off from the wall—and angle up toward the surface and kick. Take two arm strokes, and then take a breath. You should be at or beyond the 5-yard mark, more or less. Repeat until you get this step. Don't worry so much about how far out into the pool you are getting at this point. Concentrate on doing the turn in the proper sequence. But you will probably be 5 yards out if you parked your feet properly on the wall. Even a mediocre turn will get you 4 yards out.

Recapping: Order of the Flip Turn

1. Take two arm strokes without a breath going into the wall.

2. The last arm stroke is one (or two) after you cross the T on the pool bottom.

3. Your arms are at your side.

4. Keep kicking, watching the wall, with your arms at your side.

5. Flip.

6. Do a biceps-curl pull with your arms to help you flip faster.

7. Land your feet on the cross on the wall about 12 inches under the surface, with your knees bent 90 degrees.

8. Push off, and as you leave the wall, twist onto your side as though you had just pushed off the wall in a streamlined position and, at the same time, extend your arms and hands over your head and lock your thumbs together.

9. Add four to six small kicks.

10. Take two arm strokes, and breathe in your third arm stroke.

The order is important: flip, push, twist, and then kick and swim. A lot of people get the order wrong. As long as you are learning it, you might as well learn the right way to do it.

Some swimmers take one stroke after the T, and stronger ones take their last stroke before they get to the T, but people who are just starting out might need two strokes. It all depends on how much speed you have built up as you are headed into the turn and how strong you are with each stroke.

As for what to do with your feet and legs in a flip turn, a lot of people tell you to keep your knees and ankles together, but keeping them about shoulder-width apart is OK. That is how you get your best push. You are really jumping off the wall, and you would not jump with your feet together if you wanted to jump off the ground. However, keeping your feet and knees together as you flip cuts down on drag.

A big mistake is to have the feet hitting the wall at different times. Your feet should hit at the same time, shoulder-width apart.

The goal of your flip turn is to get yourself off the wall faster and to the 5-yard mark—where the lane lines change color—before you breathe.

When I was a young swimmer, we were instructed to practice turns with no breath from the flags to the wall and from the wall to the flags. That's four or five strokes in and flip, and a stroke out, with no breath. It is pretty hard to do—and it is also hard to get swimmers to do these days—but the best ones can learn to do it after a while. Remember: you'll do two strokes in and two out with no breath.

Another common mistake swimmers make when learning flip turns is to do an arm-flapping movement out to the side under the water in an attempt to stabilize during the flip. Once you do the sequence of flipping and planting your feet on the wall, you will see that, after getting your feet on the wall, you do not need to flap.

By now, you know that this flapping motion is not streamlined. It is a real drag on your speed, which is why you do not want to have it in your turn. It really slows you down.

It is easy to learn the correct arm movements once you know what to do. So, remember, both arms are by your sides as you flip; halfway through the flip, you make that biceps-curl motion to help you flip faster. Then you extend your arms into a streamlined position over your head.

Following is a more detailed description for those who need it.

Arm Mechanics for Flip Turns

1. When you get ready to make your last arm stroke before flipping, one arm will already be by your side because it is finishing a stroke, and the other will be reaching out to grab the water and flip.

2. As you finish your last arm stroke, end with that arm also by your side, and you will be ready to flip over.

3. Then you do a somersault, with your arms next to your body.

4. To help you flip faster, with your arms still by your side, turn your palms so that instead of having your thumb by your side, your pinky is by your side. Then pull your palms toward your shoulders—a quick biceps curl—both arms at the same time. That will flip you over much faster, improving the speed of your turn.

5. Your arms are now folded, with your elbows by your sides. Your palms are on either side of your face.

6. As you push off the wall, extend your hands and arms up over your head and rotate your palms back into a streamlined position—just as you did for pushing off the wall.

7. Take two arm strokes, and in the third arm stroke, breathe.

In practice, swimmers often allocate about 10 minutes at the end to work on turns. If you really want to become proficient, that is the way to do it. Take time after each workout, and do 20 turns. Do this every time until you master turns and you are comfortable doing them. Then you will be ready to start adding them to your workouts.

WORKOUT 3

In this workout, I have added some drills that help you work on turns while you are swimming. For those who want to add them to a workout, I have included flip-turn practice so you will know how to add them to future workouts.

1. Warm up—swim four 25s freestyle, resting 25 seconds, easy to moderate speed. (100) *Warm up—swim four 50s, resting 15 seconds, easy to moderate speed. (200)*

2. All levels: Swim two 50s as 25 yards 10/10 drill and 25 freestyle. Rest 25 or 15 seconds. (200) *(300)*

3. All levels: Flip-turn practice:
   • Somersaults standing in the water
   • Flipping-out drill—two 25s
   • Half a flip turn—5–10 times
   • Full flip turn—5–10 times
   • Full flip turn with push-off—5–10 times (250) *(350)*

4. All levels: Four 50-yard swims done starting in the middle of the pool, with flip turns at both ends:
   • Tread water in the middle of the pool.
   • Swim to the wall; do a flip turn.
   • Swim 25 yards, and at the other end, do another flip turn and push off.
   • Swim to the middle of the pool and rest 30 seconds maximum if possible, treading water. Repeat three times. (450) *(550)*

5. Using flip turns, do three 25s, two 50s, and one 75, all on 25 seconds of rest. Rest 30 seconds. (700) Rest and repeat, if desired, for challenge set. (950) *Using flip turns, do three 50s, two 75s, and one 100, all on 15*

seconds of rest. (950) Rest and repeat, if desired, for challenge set. (1,350)

6. Warm down—swim four 25s, easy to moderate speed, with flip turns optional at the end of each 25. (800) (1,050) *Warm down—swim three 50s, easy to moderate speed, with flip turns. (1,100) (1,500)*

CHAPTER 5

INTERVAL TRAINING: THE NEED FOR SPEED

Week 4: 45–60 minutes each session; three sessions

For this lesson, you will need:
Goggles and cap
Pace clock or stopwatch or triathlete's watch

With this week's workouts, I will get you into swimming shape. That means that you need to learn how to do several swims without a lot of rest. The goal by the end of this week is for you to do six to eight 25s if you are new, or six 50s if you are experienced, on shorter rest periods, swimming with a comfortable stroke at a comfortable pace. This is called interval training, and the various tasks are called sets.

You may have heard people say they were doing "ten 50s on a minute 15" (1:15) or "ten 50s on the 45" (:45). What that means for the first example is that they were swimming ten 50-yard distances and that every minute and 15 seconds, they started a new 50-yard swim. In the second example, they were swimming ten 50-yard distances, and every 45 seconds, they started a new 50-yard swim. This is interval training, and if you want to swim like a real pro, and particularly if you want to swim faster, you need to add it to just about every workout.

For you, a set might be four 25s and two 50s all on 25 seconds of rest. It might be followed by a set of four 50s.

If you are already in swimming condition, none of this will be new. In fact, if you have done sets before, the only thing that may make this week a challenge is that your newer, longer stroke will tire you out a little faster than your old one did. So, your goal is to get into swimming shape with your new stroke and to hold your stroke the entire time.

If you have never done interval training, the first one or two times you swim a distance will seem easy, but it gets harder as you go. You may be breathing hard. Your arms may feel tired. But you will make it because you will set your own interval times. Your goal is to just keep going and try to go as close to the same pace for the last one as you did for the first one.

This lesson brings to mind a workout that the age-group swimmers in Palm Springs used to do. Most of the swimmers were between 12 and 18 years of age. The coach called it Animal Night. The workout was to swim thirty 100s on 2 minutes, with the goal time for each 100 being no more than 10 seconds slower than the swimmer's best time ever for 100 yards. A swimmer who made all thirty got a pizza. Anybody who took more than 10 seconds plus his or her best time had to skip an interval and rest for an additional 2 minutes while everybody else swam. Nobody wanted to miss. Everybody wanted to get the pizza. However, it was hard for them to do, even though 10 seconds got added on to their best times. And these kids were in shape. If they made all thirty, the next week, they had to do them within 9 seconds of their best time.

LEARNING SPEED AND SETTING YOUR INTERVALS

If you have never done intervals, you should not try to do them as hard or as fast as you can in your first attempt. Well, you can try it, but you will be lucky to make it to four of them if you do. Notice that even the Animal Night swimmers added 10 seconds to their best time.

In swimming intervals, what you are trying to do is push your performance level a little so that after a while, you will get better and faster, and you will gain the ability to swim the same distance faster on less rest. Eventually you will also be able to swim longer sets faster. This is especially important for triathletes.

Rather than swimming sets all-out, you should try to swim them at a moderate pace, or 75 percent or 80 percent of your all-out speed, at first. In some of the workouts in Chapter 11, I will give you sets with speed percentages of 70, 75, 80, 85, or 90, or all-out. But for now, concentrate on having a good stroke for the distance you swim.

Before we do intervals, I have an experiment to help you learn the differences between speeds. After warming up, swim 25 yards as fast as you can, or all-out, and see what that feels like. Then swim one lap at what you think is about 75 percent of the all-out pace. Most people have never tried this. You now have two different speeds: fast and moderate.

In the next workout, I will ask you to swim interval sets. After picking a distance for your swim, you will swim that distance and note your time. Your swim time plus your rest time is your interval. It might be 1:30, for example, or 1:45, or 2:00. Right now, nothing is a good time and nothing is a bad time. It is just your starting point.

When you swim intervals, you swim the same distance several times, resting between swims. What makes it tough is that you never allow yourself more than the interval time for the combined swim and rest. The fourth lap is harder than the first one, even if you are not swimming your hardest—guaranteed.

If you have never done interval training, you should start with 25-yard swims. If you have done it before, you can start with 50s. Even if you have done longer distances in the past, keep in mind that you are trying to groove a new stroke, and the way to do that is to swim shorter distances and gradually increase, to prevent grooving an error.

At this point, a pace clock—or stopwatch or triathlete's watch—is essential to your workout. I will explain how to time the intervals later in this chapter. But I will not give you a specific number of seconds that you must make in order to be successful at interval training, particularly not when you are learning a new stroke. I will give you some suggestions, and you should test them against your times to see what works best for you.

You should swim hard enough that you are somewhat winded, but not so hard that you can't continue when it is time to swim another 25 or 50. If you are not nearly out of breath after two or three, then you need to swim harder or make the interval slightly shorter.

For this first time, you should give yourself at least 20 seconds of rest. That should allow you to swim several 25s or 50s without difficulty. Distance swimmers who are in shape may swim 500 yards freestyle and rest 15 seconds, and then do another two or three 500s with only 15 seconds rest between each.

SETTING YOUR INTERVAL TIME

Here is how you will set your interval time for this week.

Newer swimmers, swim 25 yards for time. Don't swim it your fastest or your slowest. Swim at a moderate rate—a little more than 75 percent of your all-out pace. Then add about 20 seconds to your time, rounding up to the nearest 5 seconds on the clock. That is your total interval time. It might be 1:30. It might be 1:10. It might be 1:45. Whatever it adds up to is your time for 25s.

If you have done a lot of swimming, swim 50 yards for time. Other than doubling the yardage, the same procedure applies: Don't swim it your fastest or your slowest; go at a moderate rate, without loafing. Then add about 20 seconds to it. Round up to the nearest 5 seconds on the clock. For instance, if it took you 60 seconds to swim 50 yards, then add 20 seconds to that, and your interval time would be 1:20 for 50s. If you took 30 seconds to do 50 yards, add 20 seconds to that, and your interval would be :50.

Here is how you determine your interval:

1. Find your time for a 25 or a 50: When the second hand is at 12 on the watch or 60 on the pace clock, push off the wall with a streamlined start and swim your distance at a moderate rate.
2. When you stop, immediately look at the second hand and see how long it took you. That is your swim time.
3. Now add a rest time to that, usually 20–30 seconds. If you need to take longer, go ahead and add a longer time.
4. Your swim time plus your rest time equals your interval.

No time is good or bad. It is just the time you are currently using. Your goal is to try to reduce the amount of time it takes you to swim a certain distance, whether a 25 or a 50 right now. Swimming intervals will help you do that. Most people aren't in training for the next Olympics, and so the most important thing is to improve over time and improve your personal best times. Even Olympic swimmers work to beat our personal best against the clock. Sometimes, when trying to swim our personal best, we get lucky and set a U.S. or world record.

Improving your time is especially important if you are competing in age-groups or in triathlons. However, if you are interested in training for the Olympics, even if it's the Senior Olympics, then learning how to swim intervals is essential, because that is how you will learn speed.

Pace clocks have a large-sweep second hand, which makes it easy for you to time yourself and swim intervals.

It is more convenient to make your intervals in 5-, 10-, 15-, or 20-second increments, just because it's easier to do the calculations. You don't want to be doing intervals on 1:23. You will go nuts trying to add that every time on the clock.

Once you get used to what you are supposed to do, it will not be a problem for you to do intervals on :55 or 1:05 or 2:45. But for simplicity, in the beginning, it's usually easier to round up to the nearest quarter minute or the nearest 10 or 20 seconds.

TIMING YOUR LAPS—EXAMPLES

When you swim intervals, you will start when the second hand is on 60 on the pace clock, or when it's on 12 on your watch. If you have a digital watch, it may allow you to set intervals.

You will swim your distance and then immediately check the clock or watch, and when your interval time ends, you will start your next swim. You will keep on doing this until you have completed the number of swims in the set.

Here are some examples—with indicators for both watch and pace clock:

1. **1:30 Interval.** If you are swimming 25s or 50s on 1:30 intervals, you will leave the wall and start a new lap every minute and 30 seconds.

- You leave the wall at the 12 or 60 for the first lap.
- You leave at the 6 or 30 for the second.
- You leave at the 12 or 60 for the third.
- You leave at the 6 or 30 for the fourth, and so on.

2. **1:20 Interval.** If you are swimming 25s or 50s on 1:20 intervals, you will leave the wall and start a new lap every minute and 20 seconds.
   - You leave at the 12 or 60 for the first lap.
   - You leave at the 4 or 20 for the second.
   - You leave at the 8 or 40 for the third.
   - You leave at the 12 or 60 for the fourth, and so on.

3. **1:15 Interval.** If you are swimming 25s or 50s on 1:15, you will leave the wall and start a new lap every minute and 15 seconds.
   - You leave at the 12 or 60 for the first lap.
   - You leave at the 3 or 15 for the second.
   - You leave at the 6 or 30 for the third.
   - You leave at the 9 or 45 for the fourth.
   - You leave at the 12 or 60 for the fifth, and so on.

4. **1:10 Interval.** If you are swimming 25s or 50s on the 1:10, you will leave the wall and start a new lap every minute and 10 seconds.
   - You leave at the 12 or 60 for the first lap.
   - You leave at the 2 or 10 for the second.
   - You leave at the 4 or 20 for the third.
   - You leave at the 6 or 30 for the fourth.
   - You leave at the 8 or 40 for the fifth, and so on.

5. **1:05 Interval.** If you are swimming 25s or 50s on the 1:05, you will leave the wall and start a new lap every minute and 5 seconds.
   - You leave at the 12 or 60 for the first lap.
   - You leave at the 1 or 5 for the second.
   - You leave at the 2 or 10 for the third.
   - You leave at the 3 or 15 for the fourth.
   - You leave at the 4 or 20 for the fifth, and so on.

6. **1:00 Interval.** If you are swimming 25s or 50s on 1:00, you will leave the wall and start a new lap every minute.
   - You leave at the 12 or 60 for the first lap and every lap thereafter.

7. **:50 Interval.** If you are swimming 25s or 50s on the :50, you will leave the wall and start a new lap every 50 seconds.
   - You leave at the 12 or 60 for the first lap.
   - You leave at the 10 or 50 for the second.
   - You leave at the 8 or 40 for the third.
   - You leave at the 6 or 30 for the fourth.
   - You leave at the 4 or 20 for the fifth, and so on.

8. **:45 Interval.** If you are swimming 25s or 50s on the :45, you will leave the wall and start a new lap every 45 seconds.
   - You leave at the 12 or 60 for the first lap.
   - You leave at the 9 or 45 for the second.
   - You leave at the 6 or 30 for the third.
   - You leave at the 3 or 15 for the fourth.
   - You leave at the 12 or 60 for the fifth, and so on.

One of those intervals will probably work for you for 25s or 50s.

Now, as you do a set, you may find that you are slower on the fourth lap than you were on the first. Your rest time may go from 20 seconds to 15 or even 10. You may get a little less rest, but as long as you are able to continue and have at least 10 seconds of rest, keep going. Interval training is not for sissies. It will make you better, and it will make you faster.

Because you have selected your own interval based on your current ability, you will probably be successful even if you have never done it before. Even so, it may not be easy the first few times you try it. It is not supposed to be easy. It is supposed to challenge your body.

If you are getting more than your expected rest time in your first attempt at swimming intervals, then shorten your interval by 5 seconds (e.g., instead of doing intervals on 1 minute 20 seconds, do them on 1 minute 15 seconds).

WORKOUT 1

Easy = 50 percent speed. Moderate = 75–80 percent speed. *Instructions for experienced swimmers are in italics for all workouts.*

1. Warm up—swim four 25s. (100) *Warm up—swim two 50s. (100)*

2. All levels: Test swim 25 yards fast and then 25 yards easy. (150) *(150)*

3. Swim 25 yards moderately for time, and then swim 25 yards easy. (200) *Swim 50 yards moderately for time. (200)*

4. Swim six 25s on your interval. When you have completed all six, rest for 1 minute. (350) *Swim six 50s on your interval. When you have completed all six, rest for 1 minute. (500)*

5. Swim four 25s on your interval. (450) *Swim four 50s on your interval. (700)*

6. Challenge set: Swim four 25s on your interval, followed by two 50s on 30 seconds of rest. (650) *Swim four 50s on your interval, followed by two 75s on 20 seconds of rest. (1,050)*

7. All levels: Warm down—swim four 25s easy, any stroke. (550) (750) (800) (1,150)

WORKOUT 2

1. Warm up—swim four 25s. (100) *Warm up—swim four 50s. (200)*

2. Swim two 25s freestyle on your interval, followed by one 50. Rest 30 seconds and repeat. (300) *Swim two 50s freestyle on your interval, followed by one 75. Rest 30 seconds and repeat. (550)*

3. Swim eight 25s on your interval, trying to make each time faster, but keep same overall interval. (500) *Swim eight 50s on your interval, trying to make each time faster, but keep same overall interval. (950)*

4. All levels: Swim 50 easy. (550) *(1,000)*

5. Challenge set: Swim three 25s on your interval, followed by 25 fast. Rest 30 seconds and repeat. (750) *Swim three 50s on your interval, followed by 25 fast. Rest 30 seconds and repeat. (1,350)*

6. Warm down—swim two 50s easy, resting 30 seconds between each. (650) (850) *Warm down—swim two 50s easy, resting 30 seconds between each. (1,100) (1,450)*

WORKOUT 3

1. Warm up—swim two 50s, resting 20 seconds between each. (100) *Warm up—swim two 75s, resting 20 seconds between each. (150)*

2. Swim two 25s, followed by one 50; repeat. Rest 20 seconds after each distance. (300) *Swim 25, 50, 75, 75, 50, and 25, resting 20 seconds between each. (450)*

3. Swim one 25 fast, record your time, and add 20 seconds to get your interval time; swim 25 easy. (350) *Swim one 50 fast, record your time, and add 20 seconds to get your interval time; swim 50 easy. (550)*

4. Swim four 25s freestyle on your interval. Rest 1 minute and repeat. (550) *Swim four 50s freestyle on your interval. Rest 1 minute and repeat. (950)*

5. Swim four 50s freestyle—25 yards 10/10 drill and 25 yards hard with good technique—resting 20–30 seconds between each. (750) *Swim four 75s freestyle—25 yards 10/10 drill and 50 yards hard with good technique—resting 20–30 seconds between each. (1,250)*

6. All levels: Warm down—swim three 50s easy, resting 20 seconds between each. (900) *(1,400)*

PART II

Chapters 6 through 8 of *Championship Swimming* deal with more advanced strokes: backstroke, breaststroke, and butterfly. The lesson format is a bit different because a new stroke is covered each week, over a three-week period, whereas the freestyle lessons spanned four weeks.

Backstroke and breaststroke can be done by most all swimmers who want to learn, and the lessons show you what you need to know to get started in those strokes. Turns used in racing are included.

We realize that most people will not want to learn butterfly. But those who are competing will need to learn it. And if you are a dedicated lap swimmer who wants a challenge, you may want to try learning butterfly. The reason butterfly is a very hard stroke to swim is that it takes a great deal of strength. Included are step-by-step instructions and some drills to help make you stronger.

If you complete all seven weeks of swimming "lessons," you will have an edge over all the other swimmers in the pool. You will know how to swim efficiently, even if you never reach world-class speed. Then, the rest of your progress is up to you. We hope you will continue to swim and enjoy the water. It is a great way to exercise and stay in shape. Swimming with effort burns the same amount of calories as running, and so if you are interested in getting or staying in shape, there is no better way to do it than swimming.

CHAPTER 6

BACKSTROKE BASICS

Week 5: 45–60 minutes each session; three sessions

For this lesson, you will need:
Goggles and cap
Kickboard (optional)

If you want to continue to learn techniques for other strokes, this week, in addition to continuing to progress with workouts, you will learn the basics of backstroke. Instead of taking four chapters for this stroke, as we did for freestyle, we will power through it in one chapter because you have already learned many of the required skills. We are confident that you will be able to do backstroke right away, because it is so similar to freestyle. That is also the reason we are doing it as your second stroke.

You will notice that the workouts get longer as you go, particularly if you are adding the challenge sets. There are two primary reasons for this. The first is that you are getting stronger with every workout, and so you are able to do a little bit more. The second is that you are adding a stroke to your repertoire, which means that you will use different muscles and so muscle fatigue is less than what it would be if you were doing the same yardage for one stroke. You will be doing some freestyle along with backstroke. By the end of the week, you will be able to do between 1,000 and 1,700 yards. If you do not feel able to complete an entire workout, cut out one set so that you have a session you can manage. Later, when you are much stronger, you will be able to do these workouts with ease.

SIMILARITIES BETWEEN BACKSTROKE AND FREESTYLE

If you have mastered freestyle, backstroke will be a snap for you.

The most significant similarity between the two is that, just as you are never really on your stomach in freestyle except between strokes, you are never really on your back in backstroke except between strokes. Having learned the reason in freestyle—that rotating your body is more efficient and streamlined than being flat—you can readily understand how the same principles will apply in backstroke.

The kick in backstroke also is similar to that in freestyle, but backstroke requires a six-beat kick. There are six kicks for each two arm strokes: one-two-three for one arm, and four-five-six for the other.

The flip turn in backstroke is identical to the flip turn for freestyle. With all that, it should be clear how learning the fundamentals in freestyle helps make learning backstroke a snap.

If you are already doing some form of backstroke, you can skip the following section, which addresses nervous swimmers—those who can swim freestyle but are a little uncomfortable in the water when it comes to doing new things. If you're ready to go on, flip ahead to "Basics for Backstroke."

ASSURANCE FOR NERVOUS SWIMMERS

The first skill you need for backstroke is the ability to float on your back. A lot of people become nervous at this prospect if they are not yet comfortable in the water. The key to floating on your back is to relax, just as you did in floating on your stomach. Floating on your back is just like lying on a bed. If you are nervous about it at all, hold on to the wall or the pool ladder with one arm at first to give you confidence that you will float easily.

To float, relax your head and lie back, looking straight up. Extend your arms straight out from your shoulders so that your body is in the shape of a cross, and bring your tummy—belly button, if you like—up to the surface.

Take a breath in, and then blow air out. You'll notice that as you breathe, your body raises and lowers in the water. If you are especially muscular, your legs may hang down 12 inches or so below the surface while you do this, but if you keep your arms extended and stay relaxed, you can pretty much hold this position for hours.

Recently my coauthor observed a woman at her first swim lesson. The woman was nervous but was determined to learn to swim. She was working on gaining confidence going under the water; she was afraid she would sink to the bottom of the pool. She didn't understand that there was no way she could stay down, even if she tried.

My coauthor and the instructor did an experiment with her in the pool to help convince her that even if she didn't do anything, she would come back up to the surface. They told her to push down on the shoulders of my coauthor—making her go underwater—and then let go. My coauthor, of course, immediately popped back up to the surface, like a cork. After doing this a few times, the woman could see that my coauthor was doing absolutely nothing but resting cross-legged in the water, and still, she popped right up to the surface.

If you are nervous about lying on your back or somehow think that you will sink when you do, ask a friend who is a good swimmer to be the "cork" for you. Trust me, corks will pop right back up to the surface, whether they want to or not.

Of course, you should never hold anyone underwater. That is dangerous and can cause drowning. But this experiment will help prove to you that you are more buoyant than you thought. It doesn't matter if you are on your back or on your stomach: you will be able to float.

BASICS FOR BACKSTROKE

Backstroke is started from a position on your back. But after you push off from the wall, you immediately roll over to your side, and your body rotates from one side to the other, just as in freestyle. Swimming flat on your back—without rotation—creates a snowplow effect, slowing you down, just as swimming flat on your stomach does in freestyle. It is much harder to swim backstroke from a flat-on-your-back-position, and getting any speed in the stroke is impossible from a flat position.

Before we proceed with the stroke mechanics, I have another experiment that I want you to do. Float on your back, as described in the previous section, with your arms out to the sides. Make sure your eyes are looking up, and push your belly button up so that it is on the surface.

Now raise your head. Notice that your hips drop down in the water immediately, and you fall out of the floating position.

What that means for swimming backstroke is that the best position for your body to be in is lying back on the water as if you are on a bed, with your eyes looking up, because that makes it easier for the rest of your body to stay at the surface, reducing drag. As you know by now, reducing drag is the swimming mantra.

The other key to making backstroke easy is to keep your tummy up, because that also helps your legs stay near the surface. A lot of people say to keep the hips up, but that's a hard instruction to follow. Keeping your tummy up is easier—a no-brainer—and when you do it, your hips come up automatically. You want your hips up because that also reduces drag. So, it's head back, eyes looking up, and tummy up.

Having said that, I acknowledge that sometimes when you swim outdoors, you have to figure out ways to swim without having the sun in your eyes. It is often helpful to wear dark goggles or even reflective goggles in these cases. You don't want to look at the sun, and after a while, you will know ways to avoid that problem.

Just as in freestyle, you spend most of your time on your side in backstroke. The rotation you used in freestyle is almost identical to that used in backstroke.

The reason you rotate, other than to reduce drag, is so that you can reach down behind you and catch deep water. If you aren't rotating, you won't be able to do it. You will be doing only about a third of a stroke if you don't rotate.

Reaching for deep water will give you power with each stroke. As a result, you will need fewer strokes to get from one end of the pool to the other. As you know, fewer strokes means less muscle fatigue. In the long run, you will be faster. So, if speed is your goal, you must learn to rotate in backstroke.

In addition, without rotation, you will be adding drag, which makes the stroke harder to do. You will be slower. You will also have a harder time keeping the stroke balanced.

For many people, it is easier to rotate in backstroke than in freestyle, mainly because your face is out of the water. Speaking of your face, your eyes look straight up, and *your head is the only part of your body that does not rotate.*

One big difference between freestyle and backstroke is that in backstroke, much of the power comes from the legs, whereas in freestyle, the arms power much of the stroke. You should think of backstroke as being 50-50 arms and legs.

Just as you are never really on your stomach in freestyle except between strokes, you are never really on your back in backstroke except between strokes. In backstroke, you rotate from one side to the other.

It's obvious that the arms move differently in backstroke. We'll analyze the proper mechanics for the arm stroke before examining the kick. The arms discussion here is divided into two parts: what your hand and arm do coming out of the water, and what they do when they are under the water. Then I'll ask you to do some drills that will get you into the right position to do backstroke easily. Finally, I'll explain how to start backstroke with a streamlined push-off and how to do the backstroke flip turn. It sounds like a lot, but as I stated before, you already learned many of the basics in freestyle—so, you're primed for success.

BACKSTROKE ARM MECHANICS

The first rules are for your hand. It's fingers together, wrist locked, thumb first out of the water, pinky-side first into the water.

You've probably never really thought about which way your hand comes out of the water or goes into the water on backstroke. Now you need to learn the right method. Remember that it's thumb up as your hand comes out and pinky in as it enters. Thumb out, pinky in.

To do the stroke, you will start with your arm by your side. With your thumb up, lift your arm out of the water, fingers together, arm straight, *no* elbow bend. Keep your arm in line with your shoulder.

As you lift your arm, rotate your wrist and arm so that your hand will go into the water pinky first. Reach over your shoulder, and as you do, rotate your body onto that side and reach into the water in line with your shoulder, hand entering pinky first.

You should now be lying on one side in the water, with your arm extended, almost like in the 10/10 freestyle drill, but your head stays straight, looking up at the sky or ceiling.

The top of your shoulder on the opposite arm should be almost right next to your chin. If you cast your eyes down, you should be able to see the top of your shoulder next to your chin with each stroke. If you do not see the top of your shoulder, then you have not rotated enough.

Now comes the hard part of backstroke, the underwater pull. Your arm is extended, and you are on your side. Press your hand down toward the bottom of the pool and reach down to grab a lot of deep water with your hand and arm. You want to reach down almost 24 inches—maybe a little less if you are smaller, and a little more if you are tall.

It's almost as though you have hooked your hand onto the water 24 inches below the surface and are grabbing onto it as if it is a handle to pull you along.

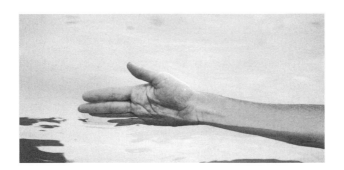

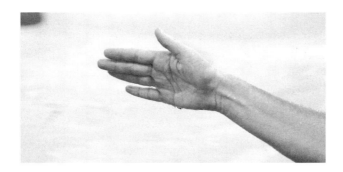

In backstroke, your wrist rotates so that your hand comes out of the water thumb first and enters the water pinky first.

In backstroke, your shoulders and body rotate under your chin, but your head stays stationary.

Bend your elbow slightly and pull the water, leading with your hand. Keep your arm out away from your body. By the time your hand reaches your waist, your elbow is bent at almost a 90-degree angle, but your elbow should not touch your waist. It should be away from your body, and your hand should still be leading. Now accelerate your hand. Push the water hard, using all the available surface of your hand and arm. Push all the way down until your hand touches your thigh, palm first, with your thumb pointing up. That is the full backstroke arm movement.

To review, here are the steps for the arm stroke:

1. Your arm is at your side; your hand is thumb up, with fingers together and wrist locked.

2. Lift your arm straight out of the water, with no bend in the elbow.

3. As you raise your arm, rotate your wrist and forearm so that your hand will enter the water pinky first.

4. Raise your arm straight up in line with your shoulder and, as your arm comes up, begin to rotate onto your side.

5. Rotate your body to the side as you reach over your shoulder.

6. Put your arm and hand in the water, pinky-side in.

7. Press down with your hand about 24 inches into the water, bend your elbow, and pull, leading with your hand.

8. Continue to pull water, keeping your arm out from the side of your body, leading with your hand, until your palm touches your thigh.

9. Your hand is now thumb up and ready for the next stroke.

In backstroke, your arms alternate in a windmill-like action so that when one arm is out of the water, the other is under the water pulling.

Once you get the movement, it is important to add the acceleration toward your thigh with your hand. When you start the underwater part of the stroke, at the top of stroke, because you are pulling a lot of water, your hand is moving more slowly. When you get halfway down, begin to accelerate, and when you are finishing, flip your hand toward your thigh. I tell young kids in my classes to think about starting out the stroke slowly and pushing the water toward their legs quickly.

In addition to giving you a long, powerful stroke, making the complete stroke—starting and finishing at your thigh with good body rotation—will help you swim in a straighter line for backstroke. I guarantee that you will swim off line if your arms are not pulling evenly. If you can make the stroke the same on both sides, you have a good chance of staying straight. If you are indoors, it is easy to pick a ceiling joist or tile to watch to help keep you straight. Outdoors it is more difficult, and you may look for trees or buildings. Regardless, if you make the same kind of stroke on both sides, you will find that you will stay relatively straight.

AVOIDING COMMON ERRORS

Just as in freestyle, certain mistakes are common in backstroke, and most of them come from not rotating. One frequently seen error in backstroke is placing the hands in the water directly above the head, with a bent elbow, instead of over the shoulder, with a straight arm. This error is easy to make, and most people who do it don't even know they are doing it.

One of the most widespread errors in backstroke is placing the hands in the water directly above the head, with a bent elbow.

Reaching directly over your head with a bent elbow is not efficient. It does not allow you to reach into the water and pull. It is wasted motion because it pushes water sideways at the beginning, instead of pulling right from the top of the stroke. If, instead, your arm is straight, you can't get your hand directly over your head. If you keep a straight arm until your hand goes in the water, you will minimize your chances of making this error.

Sometimes swimmers rotate, use a straight arm, and still manage to reach well past the shoulder. Ask someone to watch where your hand is entering the water. You may be reaching farther toward the center line than you need to. As a result, here again, you will be pushing water sideways for a while before you can begin the pull. If you are confident that you are rotating, but your hand is still going in the water almost above your head, think about putting your hands in the water as though you are swimming on the face of a clock. Instead of putting your hands in at the 12, put them in on the 1 for your left arm and the 11 for your right arm. That may help you get into a better position to enter the water properly.

Another extremely common flaw is swimming with the arm out to the side instead of straight up. This is caused by not rotating onto the side and not reaching over the shoulder. As you found out with freestyle, the shortest distance between two points is a straight line. You want to move your arm out of the water lined up with your shoulder and put it in the water in line with your shoulder, because that's the shortest distance from your thigh to the farthest extension of your arm.

A less common mistake is to cross the arm in front of the body. You can easily see where your arm is when it comes up out of the water, so just concentrate on making it line up with your shoulder until you make your rotation.

Several elbow errors also tend to occur underwater. One is to lead with the elbow instead of the hand, kind of like a chicken wing. Another is to fold the elbow too close to the body so that it is alongside the waist.

With either of these two moves, you are not getting the maximum pull from your hand and arm. To get the most from your stroke, you need to use all of the surface area of your arm and your hand to pull water.

BACKSTROKE KICK MECHANICS

The kick is a more important part of the stroke in backstroke than in freestyle. You want to maintain a straight-leg kick, just as in freestyle. In backstroke, however, you kick constantly. You need to develop a rhythm of six kicks for two arm strokes. You will find the right speed for your own stroke and kick in time, but whatever the speed, it needs to be six kicks for every two arm strokes: one-two-three for one arm pull and four-five-six for the next. You will be rotating while you are kicking.

It is important to have a straight-leg kick with backstroke. Kick from the thigh, as you did in freestyle.

If you see your knees bending and coming out of the water, you are probably not doing a straight-leg kick. A bent knee in backstroke wastes power and consumes energy. If your knee bends, you are kicking only from the knee to the foot, instead of from the thigh to the foot, which uses the largest muscles in your body—the thigh muscles—to create a powerful kick.

If your knees are coming out of the water, practice the kick by itself:

Float on your back, and put your hands either at your sides or in a stream-lined position over your head with the thumbs locked, or place a kickboard in the water and hold it over your head flat in the water with your arms extended. Make sure your head is back and that you're looking up. Even though you are not rotating, try to kick with straight legs—kick from the hip, not the knee—for one length of the pool. Don't let your knees bend or come out of the water. Bend at the ankles. Kick from the hip. You may have

The backstroke kick is from the thigh, not from the knee. It is similar to the kick for freestyle. As with freestyle, you do not want much knee bend.

difficulty the first few times, but after a couple of days, you will improve noticeably.

If you have not done this before, you will feel it in the muscles on the inside of your leg at the top of the thigh. Most of us need work in that area anyway, and so it is a good drill to practice.

Getting the rhythm and the six-beat kick may be a challenge at first, but the good news is that your face is out of the water the whole time, so it's easy to take in a breath whenever you want. You will probably find it easier to do backstroke if you create your own breathing rhythm. It may be breathing in with one arm stroke and breathing out with the other. It may be breathing in for two arm strokes and breathing out for one. It is up to you.

HOW DO I "SEE" THE WALL?

You will probably be nervous about the wall. It is easier to gauge your distance from the wall if your pool has backstroke flags. If it doesn't, then you need to find some other marker or measure to use so that you know when you're approaching the wall. One good clue is the color change of the lane lines 5 yards from the wall. If your pool doesn't have flags or lane lines that change color, then look for a ladder or a mark on the ceiling or a tree or a pole. You need a visual clue.

What you will need to do is to learn to *count how many strokes you take after the backstroke flags* or after the lane coloration change before you reach the wall. You will probably find that the number is six or seven if you are new to this, and as few as three or four if you are extremely strong and tall.

The best way to find out where you need to make your turn is to do a progression:

First, swim a length of backstroke, and as soon as you see the backstroke flags or see the coloration change in the lane lines, roll over and swim freestyle to the wall.

Next, swim another length of backstroke and, this time, take two arm strokes after the flags or lane line change, and then roll over and swim freestyle to the wall. Keep adding one backstroke arm stroke past the backstroke flags until you find out exactly how many strokes are right for you. Once you learn that, you will be able to swim backstroke with confidence to the wall.

As you improve your strength and conditioning, you may find that it takes one fewer stroke, but this change will not come as a big surprise. You won't

In backstroke, ideally, you count the number of arm strokes after you pass under the backstroke flags, which are 5 yards from the end of the pool.

go from eight strokes one time to four the next. It might go from six to five. After a while, you will figure it out from experience.

DRILLS TO LEARN POSITIONS

Let's try some drills now. The first one I will ask you to do is the 10/10 drill for backstroke. Instead of doing the 10/10 drill as you did in freestyle and rotating with your face going into the water, you will do it with your face out of the water. One arm will be by your thigh while the other is extended. This drill gets you doing backstroke in very slow motion with some extra kicking on your side. Again, the goal is to help you learn the feel of backstroke and the feel of the rotation and the pull.

Starting at the end of the pool, lie on your side, with your face above the water, one ear submerged, and one arm extended straight out and pointing toward the opposite wall.

The other arm is relaxed and resting on your side, palm facing your thigh.

Kick on your side seven or eight times, and in the last two or three kicks before you get to the tenth, with your extended hand, push down toward the bottom of the pool, grab the water, bend your elbow, and begin to pull. Remember to accelerate as your hand goes toward your thigh.

As you make your pull, lift the other hand out—thumb up—and begin to roll to the other side. Continue lifting that arm, straight up, and rotate your wrist so that the pinky side of your hand will enter the water. Lift your arm over your shoulder, finish your rotation, and place your arm straight into the water, with your hand going in pinky-side first.

You are now on your other side, with your arm extended, and kicking.

Do the same thing—kick seven or eight times, and then begin to pull with your extended hand and arm, and as you pull, rotate your body and lift the other hand and arm out of the water, thumb up. Lift in line with your shoulder, and finish your rotation as you place your arm and hand, pinky first, into the water.

Repeat for the length of the pool. Make sure your ear is in the water when you are on your side, so that you are not adding drag. Remember, if your head comes up, your legs go down. That adds drag, which makes it harder to swim and makes you slower.

In the first workout in this chapter, I will ask you to do this 10/10 drill for four 25s or two 50s. It is the best way to work on backstroke position. Don't worry about being fast. Try to do it right.

The best drill for learning backstroke is to lie on your side in the water with one arm extended, just as you did in freestyle, and kick. Then raise your arm and rotate to the other side.

If you are having trouble getting the feel of the stroke, lie on your side and pull along the lane line underwater with your hand to get the feel of what you are supposed to be doing. This drill mimics the feel of the arm pull in backstroke. So, if you are having trouble feeling it, try this drill on each side. You can do it with only one arm at a time.

Warning: The lifeguard may ask you to stop. You are never allowed to put stress on the lane lines, because these slim steel cables can't withstand much weight.

Next comes a new twist. I will ask you to do the 10/10 drill for 25 yards, but as you raise your arm out of the water, rotate your wrist so that it's thumb out and then pinky, thumb, pinky. Then lift your arm the rest of the way over your shoulder and into the water. Do 25 yards of the regular 10/10 drill for backstroke on the return lap. This drill gets you used to thinking about where your hand is in the water—thumb out and pinky in.

After that, you will be ready to modify the 10/10 drill to a 6/6 drill. Every six kicks, take an arm stroke.

Finally, you will do the whole stroke. By now, you should have the arm motion down, and you can start to concentrate on the rhythm. Instead of the 6/6 drill, the real stroke becomes a 3/3 drill. The only differences between 6/6 and the actual stroke is that you will not be doing all three kicks on the side, and your head stays eyes up. You will probably be doing two kicks on your side and rotating with the third kick each time. In the real stroke, your head stays straight, with eyes up. It does not rotate.

WORKOUT I

If you can use less rest than suggested, do so, but be sure to give your body at least 10 seconds. If you find that you need added rest—30 seconds or more—just make sure your rests are the same each time. *Instructions for experienced swimmers are in italics for all workouts.*

1. Warm up—swim four 25s easy freestyle with 25 seconds of rest after each. (100) *Warm up—swim two 50s easy freestyle with 15–20 seconds of rest after each. (100)*

2. Swim four 25s, 10/10 drill for backstroke with 25 seconds of rest after each. (200) *Swim two 50s, 10/10 drill for backstroke with 15–20 seconds of rest after each. (200)*

3. All levels: Swim one 25 as 10/10 drill, thumb out, and then rotate your hand so that it's pinky-thumb-pinky, and put your arm in the water pinky-side down. Repeat. Rest 25 seconds after each 25, if needed. (250) *(250)*

4. Swim two 25s as 6/6 drill for backstroke. Rest 25 seconds. (300) *Swim two 50s as 6/6 drill for backstroke. Rest 15–20 seconds. (350)*

5. All levels: Swim six 25s backstroke, resting 15–25 seconds. On the first 25, when you see the backstroke flags or the lane line coloration change, roll over and do freestyle to the wall. On the second 25, take two more backstroke arm strokes after the flags, and then roll over and do freestyle. On the third, take three backstroke arm strokes after the backstroke flags, and then do freestyle. On the fourth, take four backstroke arm strokes after the backstroke flags, and then roll over and do freestyle. Continue this drill until you are only one freestyle stroke from the wall. Keep taking one more stroke until you determine how many backstroke arm strokes you need after you see the flags or the coloration change. At the end of this drill, you should know how many arm strokes it takes you to get from the flags to the wall. (450) *(500)*

6. All levels: Rest 1 minute.

7. Swim two 50s—each as 25 yards freestyle and 25 yards backstroke; rest 25 seconds. Then swim one 50 as 25 yards freestyle and 25 yards backstroke, resting 25 seconds between each. (600) *Swim four 50s—each as 25 yards freestyle and 25 yards backstroke. Rest 15–20 seconds. (700)*

8. Swim four 25s—first two backstroke, second two freestyle—and then swim one 50 as 25 yards freestyle and 25 backstroke, resting 25 seconds between each. (750) *Swim four 75s, alternating 25 yards freestyle, 25 yards backstroke, 25 yards freestyle; then swim one 100 as 50 yards backstroke and 50 yards freestyle, resting 15–20 seconds. (1,100)*

9. Challenge set: Swim two 25s freestyle and two 50s freestyle on 25 seconds of rest. (900) *Swim two 50s freestyle and two 100s freestyle on 15–20 seconds of rest. (1,400)*

10. Warm do wn—swim four 25s easy freestyle. (850) (1,000) *Warm down—swim two 50s easy freestyle. (1,200) (1,500)*

STREAMLINING OFF THE WALL AND FLIP TURNS

Now that you have a good idea of how to do backstroke, it's time to add the extras that you will need to swim it well.

Just as there is a streamlined push-off for freestyle, there is also one for backstroke. In the second workout for this week, we add a streamlined push-off for backstroke, and then if you want to learn it, the backstroke flip turn. Whether you do an open turn or a flip turn, you will want to add a streamlined push-off. In a USA Swimming–sanctioned meet, to do a legal turn in backstroke or freestyle, you can touch the wall with either one hand in an open turn or just your feet in a flip turn. If you do not do a legal turn, you will be disqualified from the race. In breaststroke or butterfly, you must touch the wall with two hands.

Streamlined Push-Off for Backstroke

The goal of a backstroke push-off is to get you started on your back with some momentum. These are the steps:

1. Face the wall, and rest your hands on the edge.

2. Get ready to drop down under the water about 12 inches. Place your feet on the wall about 24 inches below the water and get ready to push off the wall.

3. Push off the wall about 12 inches under the water, and as you push, extend your arms back over your head in a streamlined position, thumbs locked, but lying on your back.

4. Begin kicking, and angle up to the surface.

5. Just prior to breaking the surface, pull with one arm and roll onto the other side.

6. Begin the stroke.

This streamlined position is how you will start every backstroke lap, no matter whether you do a flip turn or open turn.

In a streamlined start for backstroke, you lift one arm over your head, push off on your back, extend both hands and arms above your head under the water, lock your hands together with your thumbs, and begin kicking.

Backstroke Open Turn

If you do not want to learn a flip turn for backstroke, then you can use the method you learned earlier in the chapter, for workout 1, to determine how many strokes it takes you to swim from the flags to the wall. If you are racing, however, you are not allowed to turn over and swim freestyle to the wall. You need to do backstroke all the way to the wall, touch the wall with your hand, and then do a streamlined push-off to start your next lap.

If you swim a freestyle stroke in a race during backstroke, you will be disqualified. So, if you are in a race, not doing flip turns, and are not sure where the wall is, count your strokes, kick hard until you touch the wall with one hand, make an open turn, and then do a streamlined push-off to start your next lap.

If your goal is to be a lap swimmer and you do not want to do flip turns, you can continue to use the method from the last workout, in which you

In the backstroke open turn, when you near the wall, you kick and glide until your hand touches the wall, and then you do a streamlined backstroke push-off to start the next lap.

counted your strokes from the flags and then rolled over to do freestyle. You want to use as few freestyle strokes as needed—one or two—before making your turn and doing your streamlined push-off.

Backstroke Flip Turn

If you are a competitive swimmer, you will want to add a flip turn. If you are an experienced lap swimmer, you may want to add it for speed and smoothness of longer workouts. In addition, since a good flip turn gets you farther into the pool than an open turn, if you use flip turns, you will take fewer arm strokes with each length, reducing muscle fatigue.

The backstroke flip turn is almost identical to the freestyle flip turn, but after the flip, you push off on your back, not on your side. You want to go from swimming on your back to swimming on your back. So, the backstroke flip turn is actually easier than the freestyle one because there's less to do after the flip.

You already know how many arm strokes past the flags it takes you to get to the wall. Now you want to count how many arm strokes it takes so that, when you roll over, you are taking only one arm stroke past the T on the bottom of the pool and then doing a freestyle flip turn.

As soon as you cross the T and take one arm stroke, do a flip turn and push off on your back in a streamlined position, and begin kicking immediately.

A rule of thumb for adding the backstroke flip turn to your routine is to *take one fewer stroke* after the flags than you took with your open turn. On your last stroke, instead of a normal backstroke arm stroke, cross your arm over your body and over the opposite shoulder, roll onto your stomach, and pull with that arm the same way you would for a freestyle stroke and flip.

Push off on your back underwater, kicking as you go, angle up to the surface, and begin the next lap with a stroke.

If you are in competition, keep in mind that if you take more than one arm stroke going into the turn, you will be disqualified. One arm stroke of freestyle is all that is allowed during the backstroke turn. That is why you have to count your strokes and be consistent with your arm stroke. You will always know the exact formula: for instance, it's five strokes after the flags, roll, take one freestyle stroke, and flip.

As for the flip turn, like the freestyle turn, it's best to practice it at the end of a workout, swimming from the flags in toward the wall, doing the flip turn, and then kicking out. Your flip turn should get you out at about the flags.

The backstroke flip turn is much like the freestyle flip turn. You are allowed one freestyle arm stroke after you roll over before flipping. You push off on your back and begin kicking. When you come up to the surface, start your stroke.

If you are a more advanced swimmer, you may want to add the dolphin kick underwater. We will talk about the dolphin kick in Chapter 8.

I won't give you the distances for turns for world-class backstrokers, because they all do an underwater dolphin kick, which can be used for up to 15 yards or meters each length. The 15-yard or -meter rule was enacted when swimmers were able to go nearly 50 meters underwater with their turns. The IOC, the international swimming association, determined that 15 meters would be the maximum allowed.

WORKOUT 2

1. Warm up—swim four 25s easy freestyle on 20 seconds of rest. (100)
   Warm up—swim two 50s easy freestyle on 15–20 seconds of rest. (100)

2. All levels: Swim four 50s—each as 25 yards 10/10 drill backstroke and 25 yards backstroke—on 15–20 seconds of rest, according to level. (300)
   (300)

3. Swim four 25s backstroke, and then swim two 50s as 25 yards freestyle and 25 yards backstroke, on 20 seconds of rest. (500) *Swim three 50s backstroke, and then swim two 75s as 25 freestyle and 50 backstroke, on 15–20 seconds of rest. (600)*

4. Swim two 50s freestyle and then four 25s backstroke, resting 25 seconds. (700) *Swim four 50s freestyle and then two 75s backstroke, resting 15–20 seconds. (950)*

5. Swim four 25s and three 50s freestyle, and then swim two 75s freestyle as 25 yards freestyle, 25 yards backstroke, 25 yards freestyle, on 20 seconds of rest. (1,100) *Swim four 50s freestyle, and then swim two 75s as 25 yards freestyle and 50 yards backstroke, resting 15–20 seconds. (1,300)*

6. Challenge set: Swim two 25s backstroke and two 50s freestyle on 20 seconds of rest. (1,250) *Swim two 50s backstroke and two 100s freestyle on 15–20 seconds of rest. (1,600)*

7. Warm down—swim four 25s easy freestyle. (1,200) (1,350) *Warm down—swim two 50s easy freestyle. (1,400) (1,700)*

WORKOUT 3

1. Warm up—swim two 50s freestyle, resting 20 seconds between each. (100) *Warm up—swim two 75s freestyle, resting 20 seconds between each. (150)*

2. Swim two 25s and one 50 freestyle; repeat. Rest 20 seconds after each swim. (300) *Swim 25, 50, 75, 75, 50, and 25 freestyle, with 20 seconds of rest between all distances. (450)*

3. Swim one 25 backstroke fast; record your time, and add 20 seconds to get your interval time; swim one 25 easy. (350) *Swim one 50 backstroke fast; record your time, and add 20 seconds to get your interval time; swim one 50 easy. (550)*

4. Swim two 25s freestyle on your interval, followed by two 25s backstroke on your interval; repeat. (550) *Swim two 50s freestyle on your interval, followed by two 50s backstroke on your interval; repeat. (950)*

5. Swim four 50s freestyle as 25 yards 10/10 drill and 25 yards hard with good technique, resting 20–30 seconds between each. (750) *Swim four 75s freestyle as 25 yards 10/10 drill and 50 yards hard with good technique, resting 20–30 seconds between each. (1,250)*

6. Challenge set: Swim four 25s freestyle on your interval, and then swim two 50s backstroke with 20 seconds of rest. Repeat. (950) *Swim three 50s backstroke on your interval, and then swim two 75s freestyle with 15–20 seconds of rest. (1,550)*

7. All levels: Warm down—swim three 50s easy freestyle with 20 seconds of rest. (900) (1,100) *(1,400) (1,700)*

CHAPTER 7

BREASTSTROKE BASICS

Week 6: 45–60 minutes each session; three sessions

For this lesson, you will need:
Goggles and cap
Kickboard
Water noodle (optional)

One advantage of breaststroke—or "breast," as we call it—is that you can get a breath with every stroke. That makes it a favorite for many swimmers who have a difficult time learning the breathing for freestyle.

MODERN BREASTSTROKE

The way breaststroke is taught now is completely different from how it was taught 30 or 40 years ago. If you learned breaststroke in the 1960s or 1970s or even the early 1980s, you will want to learn the more modern techniques as described in this chapter. In fact, breaststroke has changed since I swam it in the Olympics in 1988. At that time, you were not allowed to put your head under the water. Now you can. So, even I have had to learn new techniques to stay current.

After I've explained each step to you, with the help of photos, I am confident that even if you have never tried breast, you will be able to swim it. It is my specialty stroke, and I like to see everyone swim it.

In their mechanics, breaststroke and butterfly, which I will cover in the next chapter, differ significantly from freestyle and backstroke. In the chapters on freestyle and backstroke, I stressed the importance of rotating your body from side to side to give you a long, streamlined stroke. In breaststroke and butterfly, your body will be back to that snowplow position that we got rid of in the first and second weeks. The snowplow position is completely wrong for freestyle and backstroke, but it's the right one in breaststroke. Since most everybody knows that position—flat on your stomach in the water—it's like getting a head start on this lesson without even trying.

In swimming breaststroke, you have to work to overcome the drag that happens as a result of being flat. You have to learn to "trick" the water into streamlining past you. It is hardest to be streamlined in breaststroke, but it is easier now that you can put your head under the water. The way we used to do it had a lot of drag.

I am very fond of breaststroke. It comes naturally to me. But some people have a difficult time with it. Plenty of great freestylers, backstrokers, and butterflyers can't do breaststroke worth a darn. Many swimmers competing in the individual medley (a race in which you have to swim all the strokes) struggle through the breaststroke portion. Because breaststroke has a different kick motion, some people have difficulty doing it, which makes swimming the stroke hard. In addition, some people have trouble with the timing.

In breaststroke, your legs push and your arms pull, working in two motions to propel you down the pool. The leg and arm movements happen at different times, not simultaneously. The arms start just before the legs, and the legs finish just after the arms at the end of each stroke.

I will teach you how to swim breaststroke so that it is as fluid and streamlined as possible. To make it easier to learn, I will separate instructions for the arm movement, the breathing, and the kick. The accompanying drills will help you feel each part of the stroke. Then you will do a drill to learn to feel the rhythm of the entire stroke. Finally, I will explain the breaststroke turn and the underwater pullout. From that point, the only thing that will separate you from success is practicing your technique and working on speed.

ARM MECHANICS: YOU GOTTA HAVE HEART

The easiest way to learn to do the breaststroke arm pull is to stand in waist-deep water and reach over a lane line. Never lean on the lane line; it's not made to take that kind of punishment. Just reach over it. If you're in a life-

Practice over a lane line
to keep your arms in
front of you.

guarded pool, the lifeguard will most likely tell you not to lean on the lane lines anyway, so this is your early warning.

A second way, if you don't have a lane line, is to put a kickboard in front of you at a 90-degree angle in the water just under your armpits. If you are a large adult, though, this may not work; you may be too big for the kickboard.

A third way is to use one of the Styrofoam noodles that children play with in the water. Put it under your arms so it acts like the lane line in the photo above.

The reason for using one of these three aids to learn the arm motion is that most people tend to focus on pulling back with their arms, bringing their elbows beyond their shoulders. That is wrong. Using one of these devices will make it impossible to bring your elbows back too far, and you can focus on "sweeping" the water rather than "pulling" the water.

If you learned breaststroke many years ago, you may have learned to pull past your shoulder area. That is not correct for modern times.

You should be able to see 99 percent of the arm stroke in front of you while you are swimming. Your hands should never be farther down than your shoulders.

In today's breaststroke,
your hands and arms
should never go beyond
your shoulders.

Your elbows should never drop down next to your waist or rib cage—chicken-wing style. If you do the arm stroke that way, you will not develop any strength through the water. Once your arms are even with your shoulders under the water, additional motion is not creating power, and it is adding too much drag for you to bring them back to the top of the stroke. As you know, drag is our enemy.

If you don't have either a lane line, a kickboard, or a noodle, you can practice by bending over in the water at the waist. Again, though, if you can practice next to a lane line, you will learn where your arms are supposed to be—and where they are not supposed to be—in a hurry.

It's easiest to think about the arm stroke as making the shape of a heart under the water. The top of the heart starts when your arms are extended, and the bottom of the heart is at the end of the pull, with your hands together, about 24 inches under the water—depending on the length of your arms—almost directly under your chin. Unless you are already a competitive swimmer, I am willing to bet that you have not been doing the arm motion that way. But that is the correct motion.

Now I want you to try to feel the shape of the arm stroke. I'll explain it in 11 steps:

1. Standing over the lane line, or with a kickboard or noodle or by bending over in the water, extend your arms in a streamlined position so that they are all the way in front of you just barely under the surface of the water, with the backs of your hands together, pinkies up.

2. Look down at the bottom of the pool but slightly in front of you, so that you can see your arm motion. Your palms face outward, and your arms are straight.

3. Separate your hands, and press outward and up slightly with your entire arm. Your thumbs are angled down, and pinkies are angled up. Push out toward the side of the pool, and then begin to draw the top of the heart with your hands, keeping your arms straight.

4. When your hands and arms are about 6 inches wider than your shoulders (less if you are a youngster), bend your elbows slightly and turn your hands as you would in freestyle.

5. Pull down for about 12 inches—almost like a freestyle motion but out at the side. You are drawing the sides of the heart now.

6. Make the point of the heart by rotating your hands and elbows so that your palms face each other.

7. Push your palms and arms together, ending about 24 inches under your chin. If you are loose-jointed and limber, you may be able to touch your elbows together at the end of the stroke. If you can't, *don't* force it. Most people are not loose enough to do this.

8. With your palms close together, push your hands forward until your arms are extended, ready for the next stroke.

The breaststroke sequence begins with the arms extended out in front, palms facing together. Rotate your palms to face out and push the water to the side.

Bend your elbows and pull the water back, with your hands facing the wall behind you. Turn your hands toward each other and bring them together in front of your chin, bending your elbows and bringing your hands together up almost to the surface. Extend your arms in front of you to start the next stroke.

This heart shape is where you get the power in your arm stroke. Even without your trying hard, your stroke may have been powerful enough to lift your shoulders and head almost out of the water. If so, this is correct. That is exactly what it is supposed to do. Don't fight that motion. That is the correct feeling for breaststroke arms. It lifts you up and forward. If you try the arm stroke by leaning over at the waist, you may feel as if you have to take a step forward when you make this stroke. You can see my legs come up with my arm pull. That is also correct if you are standing on the bottom of the pool. It pulls you forward.

The rest of the arm stroke is about minimizing drag until you can take your next arm stroke. This part is called the recovery. It gets your hands back to the top of the heart for the next stroke. Your head will go underwater for this part of the stroke.

9. As soon as your arms and palms touch at the bottom of the heart shape, keeping your hands and, if possible, your forearms together, fold your elbows to at least 90 degrees.

10. Push your hands out and up toward the surface in a streamlined position—just as you learned in freestyle—to start the next stroke.

11. Rotate your hands, pinkies up, and begin the next heart-shape pull.

The breaststroke recovery is how you get to the next stroke. You fold your elbows, push your hands together, and extend your arms. Then rotate your hands so that the palms face out, pinkies up, to start the next stroke.

This recovery motion gets you ready to start the next stroke in as streamlined a manner as possible. Later on, you will want to do the recovery part of the stroke as rapidly as you can, both to minimize drag and to enable you to start your next arm stroke as soon as possible. For now, just try to make the motion. Then learn to do it quickly.

The reason you want to make this part of the stroke fast is because as soon as you have pushed your palms together, you are done moving water. You want to get to the start of your next stroke as quickly as you can. And the fastest way is to do a fast fold of the elbows and push-out of the arms into a streamlined shape.

Many people forget to focus on the recovery, but it is extremely important. You need to do it properly, or it will slow down the rest of the stroke. The goal of the recovery is to bring your arms and hands forward and get your arms into a streamlined position as soon as you can.

The recovery is one way you try to "fool" the water into thinking that you are less flat than you are. Having your palms together and going into the streamlined position—just as you learned in freestyle—launches you forward with the minimum possible drag.

Now try to do the heart-shape pull again. Bring or "clap" your hands and arms together under your chin. Then bend your elbows to a 90-degree position and quickly push your hands out to the start. Repeat this while standing over the lane line or bending over at the waist until you are comfortable making the motion.

I know that this is totally unlike the other strokes you have done so far. If you have been doing an older style of arm stroke, it will feel different. Your hands should push out, sweep in, and then push together to make the shape of a heart.

If you are not using the lane line, make sure that you can see your arms and elbows during the stroke. If they go out of your line of vision, they are too far past your shoulders.

Once you have this basic motion down, you can work on adding more in-depth details. These are fine points to keep in mind:

- When you start the stroke, your hands are slightly under the surface, palms flat.
- Your arms are straight at the beginning of the stroke. Then you rotate your hands and elbows, so that the backs of your hands are almost together. Your pinkies are close to the surface.

- The first part of the pull is actually slightly up and out. It's as though you are reaching out and over to grab onto a glob of water so that you can pull yourself along.
- The width of your pull depends on how strong you are. You will want to be a little bit wider than your shoulders—maybe 6 inches.
- A common mistake is bending the elbows too early. You need to keep your arms straight, with your hands pushing out to the side of the pool, at the beginning part of the stroke.

CATCHING THE WATER

One crucial part of the stroke is drawing the sides of the heart. It happens about halfway between the start of the arm stroke and your shoulders.

To catch the water properly, after you have pushed the water to the sides, rotate your hands so that they are like a freestyle hand—fingers pointed down, pinkies toward the walls, thumbs toward each other. That is when you bend your elbows so that you can make a powerful pull through the water.

Pull as though you were doing a freestyle pullout at the side of your body. As you pull, lift your elbows slightly, but keep your hands down. The tops of your arms are at 45-degree angles out from your shoulders.

To finish off, turn your hands so that the palms are facing each other, and push your hands together. This last motion takes a lot of chest muscle strength, but it is an integral part of breaststroke.

A critical part of the breaststroke arm motion is catching the water.

Another common mistake in breaststroke arms is to pull back and out with the hands. The correct motion is to sweep out and then sweep in, making that heart shape. Push out; pull down at the side; push together.

As I mentioned earlier, you have to avoid bringing the elbows back too far. When you bring your elbows beyond your shoulders, they have a tendency to get "stuck" against your sides, slowing down the stroke, particularly the recovery.

Finally, there is the error of not being streamlined enough when you lunge forward during the recovery. During the recovery phase, you are actually moving water forward, which pushes you backward. The reason you don't notice that happening while you are swimming is that your legs are in the position of pushing you forward. It is important to cut down on how much water you actually push forward during the kick. You want to try to minimize the amount of water by squeezing your elbows together quickly and keeping your arms as close together as possible during the recovery phase.

BREATHING

You will have plenty of time to breathe in breaststroke. It is second only to backstroke in breathing friendliness. That makes it popular with many swimmers, even if they don't have perfect strokes.

First of all, you get to breathe with every stroke. Breaststroke used to be taught with one breath for every two arm strokes, but that method is decades old at this point. If you learned the older system, remind yourself that now you can breathe every arm stroke.

Breathing rhythm is based on the arms. As soon as your hands separate at the beginning of the arm stroke, your head starts to come up out of the

As soon as your hands separate at the beginning of the arm stroke, your head starts to come up out of the water; then you can breathe.

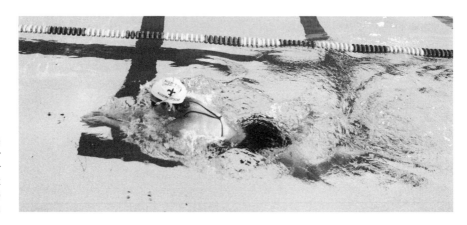

When your hands come together—as your elbows fold—duck your head under and almost lunge forward into the water.

water. Not your eyes—just the top of your head. (The next section provides more detail on head position.)

Then, while your arms are making the sweep out, your head comes out of the water and you can breathe in. When your hands come together again, as your elbows fold, duck your head under and almost lunge forward into the water with your head, hands, shoulders, and arms, getting into a streamlined position with your upper body.

When you start your next stroke—which is almost immediately—you can take another breath.

So, it's hands pull, and then head comes up; hands fold, and head goes down.

HEAD POSITION

The head position has changed since the 1980s. When I swam, the head was not allowed to go under the water. Now it's allowed. You used to be able to have your head partially under water, but now, when you are reaching for that next stroke, you are allowed to go down deeper to get into the streamlined position with your head between your arms. You already know how to do that part. It is just like the streamlined push-off position that you already learned, only you do it flat in the water instead of on your side.

When you reach out in the streamlined position, your head is slightly under the surface. Some people go deeper than others. The idea is to go just deep enough to get streamlined and completely extended.

When you take a breath, *keep your head almost in the same position it is in when you are streamlined*: looking at the bottom of pool, about 24 inches out in front of you.

When you are reaching for that next stroke, you are allowed to go down deeper to get into the streamlined position with your head between your arms.

When you come up, *you do not change position or move your head at all.* Your body will come up so that you can breathe, but your head does not move up and down. You don't want to raise your chin at all.

Recall that lifting motion of the body that you felt during the arm stroke practice. That is what will help automatically lift your head up so you can breathe.

Many breaststrokers—even good age-group swimmers—lose time in breaststroke with incorrect head position. It is an easy mistake to make.

The handiest guideline is that if you can see the end of the pool—or chairs or equipment on the pool deck or even the cross marker on the wall—before you are almost at the wall, your head is up too far and your chin is too high. You will see many swimmers raise the chin too high, look toward the end of the pool, and then take a breath and move the head back down and under. *This extra bobbing of the head wastes energy and doesn't help you accomplish your goal of getting to the wall as fast as you can.* You need to be concerned with conserving energy, so why spend energy doing something that won't help you swim any faster?

Breathing too late can also be a problem. Breaststroke is all about timing, and if you breathe late, you will end up spending too much time with your hands under your chin. This will delay your recovery portion of the stroke and slow you down.

Now practice breaststroke arms for at least two 25s, using a freestyle kick. If you are having trouble, practice over the lane line again and then try another two 25s with freestyle kick. Don't worry about going fast. It is unlikely that you will go fast at first. Concentrate on five priorities:

1. Make the heart-shape pull and the recovery.
2. Feel where the breath is as you bring your arms together under your chin.

3. Hold your head in the same position it was in when you were streamlined.
4. Pull the heart shape and breathe.
5. Fold the elbows and lunge forward.

It's pull and breathe, fold and lunge.

BREASTSTROKE KICK MECHANICS

To understand the proper breaststroke kick, you first need to discard all the conceptions you have about it. More than likely, the correct kick is altogether different from what you think or imagine or do. For example, in the past, people were taught to bring the knees up nearly under the chest. That's not done anymore. People have been told that the kick is wide, as in ballet, or that the knees turn out. Others have been instructed to keep the legs together from the knees up. None of those is accurate.

Go into this explanation with an open mind, and you'll come out with a good kick. Your goal with the breaststroke kick is to use the inside of your foot—the arch—in conjunction with the inside of your calf and thigh, squeezing them together to propel you through the water. The strength and speed of your squeezing motion will determine the power of your kick.

Just as you made the shape of a heart with your hands in the pull, you are now going to make the shape of a circle with your feet, but this time you will use the inside of your arches. The circle starts under your rear end and finishes with your legs extended behind you and your knees and feet together.

Just as in the pull, your legs move as mirror images of each other. Both legs do the same thing but on opposite sides. The motion is up, out, together—carving a circle in the water.

You may want to use a kickboard to learn the breaststroke kick. You can also brace yourself against the side of the pool, hanging on to the edge with both hands at an even height, but this does not give you the motion of the stroke, so I suggest the kickboard.

Another way is to go into deeper water and hold on to a lane line if you need to, or take a pull buoy or a float, and practice the kick vertically in the water so you can see what you are doing. Here again, it does not give you the right forward motion the way the kickboard does, but if you are having trouble figuring out where your legs should be, this is an option.

I'll describe the motion of the kick and then explain how to do it either with the kickboard or as though you were standing in the water.

Kickboard Method

Hold on to the kickboard with your hands at the top of the board. You will be at a slight angle in the water, with your shoulders higher than your hips. This is almost identical to the way your body is in breaststroke during the kick portion, which makes this a good method to use. It will feel very similar to doing the kick in a real stroke.

Here is the sequence of the kick:

1. Start with your legs together, straight out behind you, just below the surface of the water. Let your toes relax.

2. With your legs together, bend your knees up until they are at almost a 90-degree angle to your body. As you do this, lower your hips and arch your back slightly, trying to make a straight line from your chest to your knees. You do not want to bend at the hips. You want to stay flat—a straight line—from shoulders to knees.

3. Your heels should be just under the surface, with your knees bent at 90 degrees, hips down, and back slightly arched. It is OK if your knees are apart.

4. Get ready to draw a circle with your feet by opening your legs from the knee down so that you can "draw" with the inside arches of your feet. Your arches now face the wall behind you, and your big toes point to the sides of the pool.

5. As soon as you turn your feet out, separate your knees to shoulder width and start the circle—a half circle with each foot—by pushing out with your arches.

6. Try to grab the water with the inside of your feet, calves, and legs, and then, as your legs straighten, push or squeeze them together so that your toes, ankles, and knees almost touch just below the surface.

The breaststroke kick sequence begins with your legs extended behind you, close together. Your knees bend, but your body stays straight from your shoulders to your knees. Your feet angle out as your knees come apart, shoulder width for beginning students. Your feet circle out, and your legs push or squeeze together to get power and end extended behind you.

For beginners, it is important to separate the knees only as wide as the shoulders. Having the knees any wider makes it too difficult to kick and increases the amount of time it takes to get your legs around. Some great swimmers can kick with their knees slightly outside the width of their shoulders, but it is not a good idea for those who are beginning the stroke.

When you kick, glide forward, and notice the power it gives you. You will also notice an undulating motion as you kick. If you do this right, your hips will go down a little as your knees come up, and they'll rise as you squeeze your legs together. This is correct. It is not as much of a hip motion as in butterfly, but it is slightly dolphinlike. Remember that.

The power of the breaststroke kick comes from pressing the inside of your foot, the inside of your calf, and the inside of your leg against the water—squeezing it, forcing you forward. You can compare it to a plastic bottle of shampoo: squeezing the bottle causes the shampoo to shoot out, just as squeezing your legs together causes you to go forward.

Your goal is to push the water behind you. You want to keep your feet up and out as long as possible and then push the water back, starting with the inside of your arches.

Your inner thigh muscles, which you use to bring your legs together, play a major role in breaststroke.

Among the mistakes that people tend to make in the kick, the most common is failing to get the feet angled out correctly. Swimmers who typically swim a lot of butterfly, backstroke, or freestyle are used to pointing their toes. In breaststroke, the motion of the ankle is the opposite. If you kick breaststroke properly, you will actually be pulling your toes up toward your knees. You will flex them, not point them.

In freestyle, you point your toes all the time. In breaststroke, at the beginning of the kick, you flex your toes, and at the end of the kick, you point them to streamline.

An error characteristic of people who learned the kick many years ago is to bring the knees up too far under the body, even as high as under the chest.

Some instructors teach a kick in which the knees stay close together and just the lower leg moves. This is stressful on the knees. It is also not as powerful as kicking with the full length of the leg. I don't recommend it. It hurts to do it!

Another familiar fault is having the knees too wide and turning the leg out to the side so that the knees actually point to the sides of the pool instead of toward the bottom. You could call this a frog-kick style.

Some people open their knees and then kick out from the knee instead of squeezing the legs together. This is another power drainer.

A common kicking error is bringing the knees up underneath the body instead of keeping the thighs extended behind you.

And finally, there is the ever-present scissor kick, in which the legs are working like a pair of scissors—one leg is pulling down, and the other leg is pulling up, as in sidestroke.

Now that you know how to do the correct breaststroke kick, the next step is to put that knowledge into action.

Another common kicking error is making a scissor kick instead of a breaststroke kick.

Practice by doing two 25s with the kickboard so that you feel comfortable doing the kick. Then do two more.

Optional Vertical Kicking Practice

Go out into the water deep enough so that you can't touch the bottom with your feet.

Hang on to the lane line gingerly with one hand. Or just do the kick from a vertical position without hanging on. Or take a pull buoy or water exercise barbell to hang on to.

Keeping your legs together, bend your knees 90 degrees—as if you were kneeling—and then lift your heels toward your rear end.

Turn your feet out to the side, and open your knees to shoulder width. If you look down to the side, you should be able to see the sides of your feet outside of the line of your leg, knees still bent.

Now draw a circle—half with each foot—pressing against the water with the inside of your arches. Try to grab the water with the inside of your foot as you draw the circle, ending by squeezing your legs together and extending them. As you squeeze your legs together, you will pop up in the water slightly.

PUTTING THE STROKE TOGETHER

Timing is the last issue for breaststroke. The basic timing keys are that when your head goes up, your knees and legs come up. When you put your head into the water, you are squeezing your legs together and lunging forward.

This rhythm counters the drag created by having your body flat and your knees bent. The arm pull counters the drag of your knees. The kick counterbalances the drag caused by the recovery. You are streamlined under the water momentarily between strokes. The sequence is pull, kick, glide.

In more detail, you press out with your hands and raise your head to breathe; at same time, your back arches, and you bend your knees and bring your feet up. It's press out with the hands, lift the head, lift the heels.

As your feet go out wide and you are about to kick, you are bringing your arms forward. You almost lunge at that point.

When you kick—make the circle with your feet—lunge forward into a streamlined position. The kick will finish slightly behind your arms.

Think of breaststroke as a battle against a motion of two steps forward and one step back. Your goal is to get everything going forward and nothing going backward.

TIMING DRILL

While many people get the rhythm of breaststroke right away, it can be tricky for others. If you are having difficulty, try the following drill to help you get the feel of the stroke.

Take an arm stroke, and then kick and glide in a streamlined position; hold the streamline for 3 seconds before you start the next stroke. Count to three underwater during the streamline: one one-thousand, two one-thousand, three one-thousand. Now take the next arm stroke, and then kick. Do that for 25 yards.

Then, for the next 25 yards, count one one-thousand, two one-thousand during each glide.

The next 25 yards, count one one-thousand before starting each arm stroke. Keep your arms extended out until you feel your legs together and feel the glide.

When you feel the rhythm, you can speed up the tempo accordingly. There is a glide in breaststroke, but the faster you go, the less time the glide takes.

Problems with timing include trying to start the arms and legs at the same time. Remember that it's arms first and then legs. You will know if you are trying to do them at the same time because you won't make much progress in the water.

ARM AND KICK DRILLS

The drills in this section help in learning breaststroke. They are also good to use to improve your stroke. Just as the 10/10 drill works well in freestyle, these work well for breaststroke.

Arm-Strengthening Drills

- **Pull Buoy Drill.** Using a pull buoy between your legs, swim, isolating the arms. For extra work, use training paddles. Try to accelerate your arms during the recovery. This drill is difficult at first, but if you want to improve your breaststroke times, it is excellent.

- **Two-Pulls/One-Kick Drill.** Instead of swimming breaststroke as one pull and one kick, swim as two pulls and one kick. For the first arm pull, your legs are extended behind you in the water, floating. So, it's pull, pull, kick, pull, pull, kick. Swim a length or two of that to work on your pulling strength.

- **Accelerating Recovery.** Swim breaststroke concentrating on making the recovery; from the elbow fold to separating the hands, go as fast as possible.

Kick-Strengthening Drills

Kicking with a kickboard is always good for breaststroke. As discussed previously, for freestyle, the best way to kick is on your side, but using a kickboard is OK for breaststroke.

- **Two-Kicks/One-Pull Drill.** This drill focuses on the kick. The steps of the drill are pull, kick, stay underwater—or, with your hands extended in front of you, lift your head for a breath if needed—and kick a second time. It's pull, kick, kick, pull, kick, kick. When you do this drill, you should feel your hips come up out of the water in a dolphinlike motion on the second kick.

STARTING BREASTSTROKE

To start breaststroke in the water, you begin just as you did in the other strokes, with a streamline, but you add a stroke called a pull-down or pullout, used only for breaststroke. The pullout is also used at the turn.

The breaststroke pullout is basically one underwater arm pull-down and one kick, and then your head and hands come up, and you start the stroke.

At the world-class level, the pullout is particularly important because it enables swimmers to go long distances underwater without using the energy of taking several strokes. Guys will be able to go about half of a 25-yard pool length underwater with the pullout, depending on the push-off. I probably got close to that, 11 or 12 yards, with my pullout.

Steps in the Pullout

1. Duck down for a streamlined start and push off.

2. From the underwater streamlined position, you are supposed to wait until you slow down, but it works best to count at least one one-thousand, two one-thousand.

3. After that, nothing moves but your arms. From the streamlined position over your head, sweep out slightly and then in—making a keyhole shape—and finish by pressing all the way down, as in freestyle, with your hands by your thighs.

4. Count again: one one-thousand, two one-thousand. Do one regular breaststroke kick as you sneak your hands up in front of you—make an X in front of your body to slide your hands into a streamlined position over your head.

5. Angle up toward the surface, and when your head comes up, breathe and take your first stroke.

The breaststroke pullout begins with a streamlined push-off, followed by counting one one-thousand, two one-thousand.

After one underwater arm pull, count again: one one-thousand, two one-thousand. Then sneak your hands up as you do one kick, and then glide. Let your head break the surface of the water, and make your first full stroke.

In a USA Swimming meet, you can't separate your hands to start a stroke until the top of your head breaks the surface of the water, or it is considered two underwater pulls. You will be disqualified for that.

SNEAKING YOUR HANDS UP

You will need to learn this trick for the breaststroke pullout. To get your hands from your thighs to over your head, cross them in front of you, palms facing your chest, and then just slide them up quickly to the streamlined position (see photos on page 130).

BREASTSTROKE TURN

The turn in breaststroke is different from the turn for freestyle or backstroke. First of all, both of your hands must touch the wall—at the same time and at the same level. In a swim meet, failure to do this disqualifies you. So, if you are a competitive swimmer, this is something that you want to practice

Sneaking your hands up is easy. Just cross your arms in front of you, with palms facing your body, and extend your hands over your head.

the correct way from the beginning. Getting disqualified in a meet is a rough way to learn.

When I teach the turn, I try to get people to touch the wall with their palms and then make the turn. The reason for this is that some pools do not have an easy-to-grab edge, and so it is not a good idea to learn to reach for that edge because it might just be a deep wall without an edge. Most people, though, are guilty of grabbing the edge. Even I sometimes do it.

To turn, touch the wall, palms first, with your hands at the same level. If you are turning to the left, immediately after you touch with both hands, drop your left hand and do a normal streamlined push-off. If you turn to the right, drop your right hand and do a normal streamlined push-off.

This part of the turn becomes just like a freestyle push-off, dropping down 12 inches under the water and streamlining out. At that point, begin to count one one-thousand, two one-thousand, and start the pullout.

The goal in the turn is to spend as little time on the wall as possible and start in the opposite direction as quickly as you can. Pretend the wall is hot when you make your turn. Touch and go immediately.

WORKOUT 1

In these workouts, instructions for experienced swimmers differ from beginner level only for the warm-up and warm-down and in the last two workouts on the challenge sets. *The differences are in italics.*

1. Warm up—swim four 25s easy freestyle, resting 25 seconds, and then swim two 50s freestyle, resting 25 seconds. (200) *Warm up—swim four 50s easy freestyle, resting 15–20 seconds. (200)*

2. Four 25s breaststroke arms with freestyle kick. (300)

3. Four 25s breaststroke kick with kickboard. (400)

4. Four 25s breaststroke—gliding for 3 seconds between each stroke for the first 25; gliding for 2 seconds between each stroke for the second 25; gliding for 1 second between each stroke for the third 25; and swimming breaststroke the last 25. (500)

5. Breaststroke arm drill—two 25s or one 50 done as two arm pulls, one kick. Repeat. (600)

6. Breaststroke kick drill—two 25s or one 50 done as one arm pull, two kicks. Repeat. (700)

7. Swim your choice of strokes as follows: two 25s, two 50s, two 75s. (1,000)

8. Challenge set: Swim two 25s breaststroke, two 25s backstroke, and two 50s freestyle, resting 15–25 seconds. (1,200)

9. Warm down—swim four 25s or *two 50s* easy freestyle. (1,100) (1,300) *(1,100) (1,300)*

WORKOUT 2

1. Warm up—swim four 25s easy freestyle, resting 25 seconds. (100)*Warm up—swim two 50s easy freestyle, resting 15–20 seconds. (100)*

2. Two 50s breaststroke—gliding for 3 seconds between each stroke for the first 25; gliding for 2 seconds between each stroke for the second 25; rest. Swim breaststroke for the next 50, gliding for 1 second between each stroke for the first 25 and swimming breaststroke for the second 25, resting 15–25 seconds. Repeat. (300)

3. Four 25s—as 25 back, 25 free, 25 breast, 25 free; three 50s—as 50 back, 50 breast, 50 free; and two 75s—each as 25 back, 25 breast, 25 free. Rest 15–25 seconds, according to level, between each. (700)

4. Four 25s breaststroke kick. (800)

5. Two 50s freestyle and then four 25s breaststroke, resting 15–25 seconds as needed. Repeat. (1,200)

6. Challenge set: Swim two 25s freestyle and two 50s breaststroke, resting 25 seconds. (1,350) *Swim two 50s freestyle, two 50s breaststroke, and two 50s freestyle, resting 15–20 seconds. (1,500)*

7. Warm down—swim four 25s or *two 50s* easy freestyle. (1,300) (1,450) *(1,300) (1,600)*

1. Warm up—swim four 25s easy freestyle, resting 25 seconds. (100) *Warm up—swim two 50s easy freestyle, resting 15–20 seconds. (100)*

2. Four 50s breaststroke—gliding for 1 second between each stroke for the first 25 yards and swimming breaststroke for the second 25 yards. Rest 15–25 seconds, according to level. (300)

3. Four 25s—as 25 free, 25 breast, 25 breast, 25 free; three 50s—as 50 breast, 50 free, 50 breast; and two 75s—each as 25 back, 25 breast, 25 free. Rest 15–25 seconds, according to level, between each. (700)

4. Four 25s breaststroke kick. (800)

5. Two 50s freestyle and then four 25s breaststroke, resting 15–25 seconds as needed. Repeat. (1,200)

6. Challenge set: Swim three 50s breaststroke, resting 25 seconds. (1,350) *Swim one 50 freestyle, three 50s breaststroke, and two 50s freestyle, resting 15–20 seconds. (1,500)*

7. Warm down—swim four 25s or *two 50s* easy freestyle. (1,300) (1,450) *(1,300) (1,600)*

CHAPTER 8

BUTTERFLY BASICS

Week 7: 45–60 minutes each session; three sessions

For this lesson, you will need:
Goggles and cap
Fins
Kickboard

Butterfly is a beautiful stroke to watch when it is done correctly. It mimics the movement of dolphins and whales, undulating up and down above and below the surface of the water. If you can get that rhythm into the stroke, you will be well on your way to understanding how to swim it.

The stroke is called butterfly because your arms make a circular type of motion—half in the water and half in the air—almost like the shape of butterfly wings. Though it is exciting to watch, butterfly is also an extremely difficult stroke. Most people—even most people who swim miles of laps—never swim it. One reason is that it takes a lot of strength and power to swim it efficiently. However, all competitive swimmers learn it. The degree of difficulty notwithstanding, you can learn it, too. Who knows? You may become a world-class butterflyer.

I think the main cause of trouble with learning butterfly is having to move both arms at the same time. You are starting from over your head and pulling toward your hips and then lifting your arms out of the water and over your head, time after time. It is hard enough to make that movement on land. Stand up and try it. In butterfly, you are making that movement plus kicking two times with your legs for every arm stroke. But let's not get ahead of ourselves. The way to learn butterfly is to go step by step, just as you did with the other strokes. With practice, you'll be able to swim it.

Practicing butterfly is the only activity for which I recommend using fins. Fins come in many sizes—some very long and some very short. The long fins will allow you to move more water without having to work so hard. The long ones are great for beginners learning butterfly for the first time. Long fins, if you have them, make it easier at first, but if you start with long ones, you will probably want to switch to shorter workout fins later so that you can practice the kick properly. Starting with workout-size fins is fine. I would not use Zoomers (short, heavy fins) to try to learn butterfly. The reason to use fins is to provide some additional leverage for your body, and Zoomers do not have a long enough fin to do that.

I will explain the stroke in stages: the movement, the kick, the arms, breathing, the timing, the turn, and the push-off.

UNDULATING LIKE DOLPHINS AND WHALES

The first thing to learn in butterfly is the undulation. Whales and dolphins have flat tail fins, which they move up and down in the water to propel themselves. You will make that same kind of motion from the hips down, using your feet as the tail fin.

I suggest using fins to practice the undulation. Instead of practicing on the surface of the water, the best way to practice and get the feel of the undulation is to do it underwater. If you try to practice on the surface, you will not be resisting against the water on the up kick, and you will not learn the proper feel.

To start the undulation, get into a streamlined position under the water, with your arms over your head. Then, keeping your feet and legs close together, with your toes pointed, move your legs and feet as if they are a giant whale tail. You will bend your knees as you undulate. This is correct.

In the undulation, when your arms and head go down, your hips and legs go up. When your legs go down, your arms and head come up. As you will see, your hips are very active in butterfly. When you start actually swimming butterfly, your hips will come out of the water on every stroke.

Practice undulating, trying to make a sideways S in the water:

~~~~~~

In the butterfly kick, your hips go up and down, and your feet follow.

Work on the feel rather than on speed. The kick will come naturally as you make this undulation. Try to be long, loose, and flexible as you go. Come up for a breath when you need to, but keep going, so that you learn the feel of the stroke.

At this point, you shouldn't worry about technique except that when you kick down with both feet at the same time, it should force your hips up. Your feet will follow, coming up after your hips do.

When you kick up, your head, shoulders, and arms will come up. That is the correct motion and rhythm.

Using fins will make the movement easier and faster, and you may find that you can do the undulation with ease. The stroke is hard enough to learn; you might as well enjoy this as the easy part.

BUTTERFLY KICK MECHANICS

Once you have mastered the undulation, the next step is to work on the kick. There are two kicks for every arm stroke, and you have to practice the movement to execute it properly.

In the kick, the legs are together, and they move up and down together. Your legs don't have to touch, but they should be close to each other. The toes are pointed but relaxed.

Many people focus on just the kick down, but that is only half of the kick. In butterfly, there is a lot of power on the upstroke as well as on the downstroke.

When you are learning, let your legs float up, and then kick down. Whales and dolphins actually have more power on the upstroke than they do on the downstroke. So do good butterflyers.

The butterfly has a down kick followed by an up kick. When you kick down with your lower leg, your hips will come up. When you kick up with your lower leg, your hips drop.

To practice the kick, stick with shorter distances—25 yards—at first. It is a tiring kick to learn, but you will be able to do 25 yards. To start, you can try it with a kickboard, but the very best way to practice butterfly is by kicking on your side, as you did in freestyle in the 10/10 drill. You just lie on your side, with your body underwater, one arm extended, and your face out of the water. You can also do it completely underwater; however, when you are starting, you will probably want to do this with your face out of the water, just because at first, doing the kick will make you want to breathe often.

The advantage of practicing the kick on your side is that you can practice the upstroke more effectively. When people use a kickboard for the butterfly kick, they tend to practice just the downstroke, and the upstroke gets lost.

A big difference between the butterfly kick and the freestyle kick is that when you do the butterfly kick, you will bend your knees. In freestyle, there is hardly any bend in the knees, and you are always using the whole leg. In butterfly, you are using the legs to create leverage. However, when you kick up behind you and when you kick down, the last bit of kick is with the whole leg.

Although I have emphasized bending your knees and keeping your toes pointed and your legs moving close together, much of the focus in the butterfly kick is on the hips. The goal of the kick is to get the hips up so that they don't cause drag and so that they participate in the undulation that helps propel you through the water. When you kick and when you practice kicking, you should be concerned with where your hips are, not with your feet and knees.

Don't even think about trying to add the arms until you have a good kick going. As challenging as the kick is, the arms are more so. That means the kick needs to be nearly second nature before you add the arms.

BUTTERFLY ARM MECHANICS

Before you try to do butterfly arms, it helps to picture butterfly arm mechanics as being similar to freestyle, but with a straight-arm recovery. It's like doing two freestyle strokes at once with both arms moving.

There is a lot going on under the water in butterfly that gives it power. It takes a while for most people to get the correct arm movements because the important component is completely below the surface of the water.

In addition, there is the undulation movement, which is produced in large part by the arm stroke. When your hands go into the water, you go down, and when your hands are finishing, you are coming up. That's what creates the look of undulation over and under the water. However, your entire body is undulating during the stroke, going down and then up in sequence as you kick.

The most effective way to learn the arm mechanics is to first read through the sequence and moves and study the photos. Then, as you did when you first learned arm movements for breaststroke, you can bend from the waist and try the arm movement for butterfly, to get the idea. Later in the chapter, I will give you drills to help you put the arms and legs together.

ARMS STEP-BY-STEP

In butterfly, your arms enter the water extended over your head, straight out in front of you and in line with your shoulders. Your hands have the thumbs pointing down, pinkies pointing up. Elbows face the side walls of the pool.

As soon as your hands enter the water, you press down and sweep out slightly with your hands and arms, similar to the move you made in breaststroke. Your arms stay straight, and the sweep goes about 6 inches outside your shoulders—not very wide; more down than out—about 12 inches under the water.

Then you turn your hands so that your palms face the wall behind you. This should be just like a freestyle stroke. At that point, you will start to bend your elbows and continue to pull.

In the underwater position, the hand points toward the back wall, like a freestyle stroke, during the middle of the pull.

Butterfly happens so fast that it is hard to see the position of the arms under the water, but this photo shows them. The hands are about 6 inches apart.

When your arms and hands get to about chest height, bring your hands in so that they are about 3 to 6 inches apart, depending on your size.

At this stage, your elbows will be pointed out toward the side walls, and your fingers will be pointing toward each other, palms facing the back wall or your hips.

You have now made a half-circle arc with each hand, starting with your hands extended and thumbs pointing down, and ending with your fingers facing each other. Because the key to breathing in butterfly is this keyhole-shape move of bringing your hands toward each other halfway through the pull—when they are even with your chest—it is an important move to practice. This move also lifts your upper body slightly out of the water and makes it easier for you to get a breath.

To complete the arm stroke, you sweep your hands and arms back out toward your hips and finish, ending with your hands next to your hips and your palms pointing toward the sky, just like the finish of a freestyle stroke, pressing back and up and lifting them out of the water.

To start the next arm stroke, instead of bending your elbows to bring your arms out as you would in freestyle, keep your arms straight, flying them up out of the water and reaching over your head in line with your shoulders, thumbs down, as they enter the water to start the next stroke.

Be sure to finish the stroke all the way until your arms are straight.

Then, when you reach over the water, get your arms just barely over the surface but keep them straight.

The beginning of the butterfly arm is similar to breaststroke, sweeping out and then pulling, and then it switches to be more like freestyle.

The butterfly arm stroke ends with your palms pointing up toward the sky. Then sweep your arms and hands out by your hips, and bring your arms—keeping them straight—out and over the water, where they enter thumbs down, shoulder-width apart.

Errors that you inevitably see with butterfly arms include swimming the stroke with bent elbows at the recovery. This means that the arm stroke has not been completed, because at the completion of the stroke, the arms are extended and straight. Once your arms are finished with the stroke and you are reaching forward, it is OK to bend your arms slightly, but extend them again when you reach forward for the next stroke, so that you can grab for the most water when you extend.

Some people put their hands in the water too wide or too narrow. The hands should enter the water in line with the shoulders.

You may also catch swimmers putting their hands in the water with the thumbs facing each other. This wastes time in getting to the sweep motion of the stroke. The hands should enter the water thumbs first. There is no

The hands should enter
the water thumbs first.

sense in adding time to the stroke when learning to do it the right way will
save you time.

As I mentioned, the most obvious difficulty of butterfly is having to move
your arms in concert. Even on solid ground, it's awkward to swing both arms
over your head as you must do in butterfly.

TIMING FOR BUTTERFLY BREATHING

Timing is essential for adding breathing to butterfly. In the actual stroke, you
breathe every other arm stroke. Said another way, you do two arm strokes
for every breath. One reason you do this is that when you take your head
out of the water, it makes your hips drop, causing more drag. It would be
ideal to take one breath for every three arm strokes, but not many people
can keep that up. It's just too taxing.

When you start your pull, you are lunging forward and moving your head
forward under the water.

As you bring your hands back, bring your chin up to the surface, but never
have more than your face out of the water. This is when you take a breath.

Trying to lift more of your body out of the water is harder, and many people make this mistake. Another error people make is breathing too late in the
stroke, when the arms are finishing the stroke. When in doubt, try to breathe
earlier rather than later. As your hands pass in front of your face, you move
your chin up toward the opposite wall to breathe.

As your hands pass under your body, you should have your chin on the
surface of the water, facing the opposite side of the pool.

To breathe, as your hands pass under your body, lift your chin so that it rides on the surface of the water, facing the opposite end of the pool.

As soon as your arms are extended and you begin to bring them up out of the water, your chin starts to go down.

So, when you are halfway through the arm pull, your head comes up, and when your hands finish the stroke and reach for the next one, your head goes down.

The kick in butterfly helps with breathing and amplifies the power of the stroke. There are two kicks for every arm stroke: one kick is at the beginning of the arm stroke, as your hands enter the water, and the second kick is when your hands are at the hips.

Most people—not just novice swimmers—have a tendency to do only one kick. Strive to avoid that mistake. The second kick has to happen, because that helps get your arms out of the water and helps you get your breath.

KICK AND ARM SEQUENCE

In butterfly, as in breaststroke, timing is everything. These steps will help you get the correct timing sequence.

1. Kick down as the hands push past the hips. This helps get the upper body and arms out of the water to reach for the next stroke and to breathe.
2. Kick up as the arms reach over the water.
3. Kick down as the arms enter the water. The hips will come up to the surface as the arms extend below it.
4. Kick up as the hands and arms pull.
5. Kick down as the hands push past the hips.

A side view of the butterfly shows the sequence of a stroke. Kick down and the hips come up as the arms reach under the water. Kick up as the arms pull back under the water. Kick down as the arms come out of the water. Kick up as the arms "fly" around. Kick down as the arms and hands enter the water.

PUTTING IT ALL TOGETHER

When you swim butterfly, think of yourself as skimming along the surface as you undulate. You want to use the undulation of the stroke to help keep you within a certain water depth. While you will go up and down somewhat, when you actually put the stroke together, you want to contain the up-and-down movement, because the more time you spend going up and down in butterfly, the less time you are spending going forward. Also, the more time you spend going up and down, the more drag there is on your body.

Now that you have tried the undulation and practiced the kick, and perhaps given the arm movement a whirl, you're set to put them all together. I will give you several drills to help you learn how to do that. You will need to have patience to let your body become strong enough to do butterfly, but if you follow along, it will happen. Most people are not wonderful butter-flyers the first few times they attempt it. It takes many laps of practice to get it right, more laps to swim a 25, and tons more on top of that to be good.

Rocket Butterfly Drill

The drill I have everyone do first is the rocket butterfly. It's called that because you come out of the water like a rocket lifting off—then you dive back under the surface.

Push off the wall, come up out of the water, take a breath, and plunge back into the water, arms first, diving down under the surface again. In a shallow pool, you can put your feet on the bottom and then really rocket up. Obviously, in the deeper end, you dive down only a couple of feet and then head back up to the surface. This drill helps you learn where and how the arms enter the water and helps you focus on diving down and out in front of your body. Your hips will come up naturally when you do rocket butterfly.

Stroke Drills for Butterfly

I am suggesting a series of stroke drills for learning butterfly because it is very difficult to start with trying to do the whole stroke. These drills get you started with the mechanics and feel and can be done fairly easily by most people, whereas few people can do the whole butterfly stroke at the outset. Age-group swimmers don't start with the whole stroke. They begin with the kick and then move on to the rocket butterfly, and then drills, and finally the full stroke.

You can use fins for these drills initially. Later, when you are stronger, you will want to do the drills without fins because, unfortunately, the only way to learn to swim butterfly is to swim it. So, first, use the fins for the drills, and don't even try the whole stroke. Next, try the drills without wearing fins and, at the same time, start trying the whole stroke using the fins. Then, finally, you will be able to try the whole stroke without the fins. Even after that, for sessions in which you're practicing butterfly, you may want to use fins at least on occasion. If you are an age-group swimmer, your coach will have a progression that works for you.

After you have mastered the drills, the only thing between you and but-terfly is swimming it.

One-Arm Butterfly

This drill is just what the name says. You do it with only one arm. What it teaches you is the butterfly stroke rhythm—the timing of the arms with the kicks. You breathe every two arm strokes because that is when you breathe in butterfly.

When you do one-arm butterfly, try to use an arm movement that is as close to a real butterfly arm movement as possible, fingers pointing to the wall in front of you.

Do one down kick as your arm reaches and extends fully under the water; do an up kick as your hand goes underneath your body; and do the second down kick as your hand nears your thigh before you take your arm out of the water for your next arm stroke. Another way to think of the timing for the second kick is that the down kick and the final thrust of your hand happen at the same time.

Practice by doing 25 yards with your right arm and then 25 yards with the left, or vice versa.

Alternating-Arm Butterfly: The 3-3 Arm Drill

This is similar to the one-arm butterfly, but you switch arms as you go down the pool. Instead of using the same arm for all 25 yards, do two arm strokes, breathe, do a third arm stroke, and then switch arms with the underwater pull. Take a breath on the second-arm side as you reach over your head, and do two more arm strokes on that side, breathing with the second stroke, and keep going in that manner.

Do this drill for 25 yards. Rest if you need to, and then do another 25 yards.

3-3-3 Drill

Next in the progression for butterfly is to put the stroke together. Again, when you first try this, you may do better with fins.

Take three arm strokes with one arm, followed by three arm strokes with the other arm, and then three real butterfly arm strokes using both arms. Do the kicks at the right place in the stroke for both the one-arm strokes and the full strokes.

Try to do the 3-3-3 for 25 yards. Rest and repeat.

2-2-2 Drill

This is identical to the 3-3-3 drill except that, instead of taking three strokes with each arm and then three full strokes, you will do two of each.

Try to do the 2-2-2 for 25 yards. Rest and repeat.

1-1-1 Drill

This is identical to the 3-3-3 and 2-2-2 drills except that the sequence is one arm, the other arm, one full stroke; one arm, the other arm, the full stroke; and so on.

Try to do the 1-1-1 for 25 yards. Rest and repeat.

One-Arm, Six-Kicks Drill

In this drill, you will combine the arms with a lot of kicking. You start with one full two-arm stroke and then go under the water and do six kicks; come up and do a full two-arm stroke, and go under and kick six times again; and so on.

Do 25 yards.

15 Fly plus 10 One-Arm Drill

This is a progression to get you up to 25 yards of butterfly.

Instead of trying 25 yards of butterfly all at once, try to swim slightly more than half the pool—about 15 yards—with butterfly and then change to a one-arm drill for the last 10 yards, using either arm. Rest and repeat—using the other arm for the one-arm portion.

4-4 and Fly Drill

In this drill, swim four strokes with your right arm and then four with your left arm; finish the rest of the pool length with the full butterfly stroke.

25 Yards Butterfly—Fins

Completing all the stroke drills might take several weeks of practice—doing a little at a time—but once you've been able to do them all, you should be ready to try your first 25 yards of butterfly with fins. It will probably not be difficult for you to make the progression to this step.

Once you have made the progression with fins, you will need to try to make the progression without fins. Now you are beginning to understand why butterfly is hard!

Do the same drills in the same order without fins, and at the end of the progression, you should be ready to swim your first 25 of butterfly without fins. It will not be effortless by any means, but you should be equal to the challenge.

BUTTERFLY TURN

The turn for butterfly is similar to the turn for breaststroke. You must make a two-hand touch on the wall, and immediately after you touch, you drop under the water about 12 inches and push off the wall in a streamlined position.

Then, you start a quick underwater dolphin kick. With this kick, you make smaller, faster kicks than you would normally do in butterfly. You don't want too much up-and-down movement. You are kicking fast as you angle to the surface.

Freestylers and backstrokers also use this kick underwater after turns, which is legal. It is a fast kick, and that is why freestylers and backstrokers use it off the wall after flip turns. The underwater kicks in butterfly are faster than the freestyle kick because you have a little more force, since you are going up and down with both feet, like a giant fin.

As with backstroke, you are allowed 15 yards under the water in butterfly, but in reality, butterflyers do not stay under the water more than 8 to 10 yards.

PATIENCE, PATIENCE, PATIENCE

Learning butterfly can take a long time. There are plenty of great swimmers who do not do butterfly very well. Many swimmers intentionally skip it in workouts. They think, why should I put myself through that torture? It is an energy-consuming stroke. It is full-body exercise. It is hard on the back and hard on the shoulders. That makes it challenging.

In the following workouts, I have not made the distances as long as in the workouts for the other strokes, because butterfly consumes so much energy.

I will start you off with other strokes and add some butterfly drills to demonstrate how the progression to full butterfly works. That will show you how to add butterfly to your own workouts. In addition, after you do butterfly work, whether drills or the full stroke, it is a good idea to swim some easy 25s, 50s, or 100s to help reduce the lactic acid buildup. That will keep you from getting stiff after a butterfly workout. Of course, you should always warm down, but doing some easy swims after you practice butterfly will decrease the likelihood of stiffness.

WORKOUT I

Instructions for experienced swimmers are in italics for all workouts.

1. Warm up—four 50s free; 20 seconds rest. (200) *Warm up—four 75s free; 20 seconds rest. (300)*

2. All levels: One 25 fly kick underwater; rest 15 seconds. (225) *(325)*

3. All levels: One 25 rocket butterfly; rest 15 seconds. (250) *(350)*

4. All levels: One 25 fly—right arm; rest 15 seconds. (275) *(375)*

5. All levels: One 25 fly—left arm; rest 15 seconds. (300) *(400)*

6. All levels: One 25 fly—3 right/3 left/3 full strokes; rest 15 seconds. (325) *(425)*

7. All levels: One 25 fly—2 right/2 left/2 full strokes; rest 15 seconds. (350) *(450)*

8. All levels: One 25 fly—1 right/1 left/1 full stroke; rest 15 seconds. (375) *(475)*

9. All levels: One 25 fly; rest 15 seconds. (400) *(500)*

10. Six 50-yard kicks—all with fins, on side; rest 20 seconds. (700) *Eight 50-yard kicks—all with fins, on side; rest 20 seconds. (900)*

11. Four 100s—25 fly drill/75 free; rest 20 seconds. (1,100) *Six 100s—25 fly swim/75 free; rest 20 seconds. (1,500)*

12. Twelve 25s—1 fly fast/3 easy free; rest 15 seconds. (1,400) *Sixteen 25s—1 fly fast/3 easy free; rest 15 seconds. (1,900)*

13. All levels: Warm down—one 100 easy. (1,500) *(2,000)*

WORKOUT 2

1. Warm up—one 200 free. (200) *Warm up—one 300 free. (300)*

2. All levels: Eight 50s—25 fly kick underwater/25 rocket fly; rest 15 seconds. (600) *(700)*

3. Twelve 25s—streamline and fast dolphin kicks to the surface and two fast butterfly strokes, then easy freestyle to the wall; rest 15 seconds. (900) *Sixteen 25s—streamline and fast dolphin kicks to the surface and two fast butterfly strokes, then easy freestyle to the wall; rest 15 seconds. (1,100)*

4. All levels: Two 50s free; rest 15 seconds. (1,000) *(1,200)*

5. All levels: One 25 fly—3 right/3 left/3 both. (1,025) *(1,225)*

6. All levels: Two 50s free; rest 15 seconds. (1,125) *(1,325)*

7. All levels: One 25 fly—2 right/2 left/2 both. (1,150) *(1,350)*

8. All levels: Two 50s free; rest 15 seconds. (1,250) *(1,450)*

9. All levels: One 25 fly—1 right/1 left/1 both. (1,275) *(1,475)*

10. All levels: Two 50s free; rest 15 seconds. (1,375) *(1,575)*

11. All levels: One 25 fly swim. (1,400) *(1,600)*

12. All levels: Warm down—one 100 easy. (1,500) *(1,700)*

WORKOUT 3

1. Warm up—four 75s free; rest 15 seconds. (300) *Warm up—four 100s free; rest 15 seconds. (400)*

2. All levels: Eight 25s—odd: rocket butterfly; even: kick underwater. Rest 20 seconds. (500) *(600)*

3. Four 75s—fly kick with board and fins, each 25 faster; rest 20 seconds. (800) *Six 75s—fly kick with board and fins, each 25 faster; rest 20 seconds. (1,050)*

4. Two 25s fly with fins; rest 15 seconds. (850) *Four 25s fly with fins; rest 15 seconds. (1,150)*

5. All levels: One 50 easy free; rest 15 seconds. (900) *(1,200)*

6. All levels: One 25 fly; rest 15 seconds. (925) *(1,225)*

7. All levels: One 50—25 fly/25 back; rest 15 seconds. (975) *(1,275)*

8. All levels: One 75—25 fly/25 back/25 breast; rest 15 seconds. (1,050) *(1,350)*

9. All levels: One 100—25 fly/25 back/25 breast/25 free; rest 15 seconds. (1,150) *(1,450)*

10. All levels: Warm down—one 100 easy. (1,250) *(1,550)*

PART III

Chapters 9 through 11 of *Championship Swimming* include terms, exercises, and workouts.

Chapter 9 has information you may need if you decide to join a team, as well as sources for equipment and additional swimming information—such as where you can find a swim team to join, no matter your age or ability level.

Chapter 10 has swimming-specific exercises, including some that are probably new to you as well as some old standbys. They are old standbys for a reason. They work.

Finally, Chapter 11 includes 12 additional workouts, enough to keep you going for another month without repeating a session. One reason for doing different workouts is to keep your body from getting lazy, which happens when you do the same workout all the time. Variety keeps your body working hard and wondering what's next, which helps you improve.

CHAPTER 9

TERMINOLOGY, TEAMS, AND SOURCES

I've covered many of the basics in the preceding chapters, but the swimming world uses additional terms with which you should be familiar. This chapter explains some of the specialized terminology and techniques you are likely to encounter as you advance in the sport. I've also provided some sources for finding a team, no matter what your age, and purchasing equipment.

TERMS AND TECHNIQUES

Resting and Tapering

Before any big swim meet, most coaches lessen the degree of difficulty and length of the practice sessions for their swimmers. If you are training on your own, you should do the same. Whether you are preparing for a triathlon or the district swim meet, you will need to modify your schedule to rest and taper. Tapering means that you gradually swim shorter workouts so that when you get to the day of your big meet or your big event, your body is rested and more than ready to go.

IMs

We have not really touched on IMs—individual medleys. The IM is an event in swimming that includes all the strokes. It starts with butterfly and is followed by backstroke, breaststroke, and freestyle. In age-group races in 25-yard pools, the IM for ages 7–8 is 100 yards, which means that each participant swims 25 yards of each stroke. At age-group 9–10, the distance increases to 200 yards, with each swimmer doing 50 yards of each stroke.

In world-class swimming, competition is in 200-meter and 400-meter IM. The 400-meter IM is the "decathlon" of swimming, because a swimmer has the formidable task of doing 100 meters of each stroke.

In IMs, the turns are somewhat different. Butterfly-to-backstroke is easy because you finish butterfly with a two-hand touch, push off on your back, and start backstroke. In the backstroke-to-breaststroke turn, you must touch the wall with your hand while you are still on your back and then push off on your stomach for breaststroke. For breaststroke-to-freestyle, you make a two-handed touch, drop one hand, and perform a streamlined push-off. The second turn in this series, backstroke-to-breaststroke, is the trickiest.

Relays

Relays are exciting, as anyone who has watched the Olympics can attest. Relays are no less exciting in an age-group swim meet. Just ask the kids and coaches who are yelling for their teams on the pool deck!

Relays are often the last events. In meets in which points are given for each place, the relay results often determine which team wins the meet.

There are two kinds of relays in swimming: freestyle and medley. Four swimmers participate in relay events. The freestyle relay is just what it sounds like—all freestyle. The medley relay has a specialist from each stroke. It starts with the backstroke and is followed by the breaststroke, butterfly, and freestyle.

In relays, it is vital not to start the next leg of the relay until the swimmer in the water has touched the wall. Also, once the next swimmer is in the water, it is the job of the swimmer who just finished to get out of the water. Jumping back in can disqualify the team.

To learn how to execute a relay start with a dive, age-group swimmers often get set on the diving block and then extend their arms in front and use their hands to follow the hands of the swimmer in the water until that swimmer touches the wall. As the swimmer in the water gets closer, the swimmer on the block bends over more and more toward a starting position. Then, as the swimmer on the block sees the touch, he or she is in the ready position and quickly dives into the water to start the next leg of the relay.

Racing Dives

If you are a workout swimmer and not competing, you do not have to learn racing dives. If you are in competition, you will want to learn a racing dive.

The purpose is to get you started going through the water faster than you can in a streamlined push-off. The racing dive is a shallow dive, more out than down. In competition, you do a racing dive from a diving block, not from the edge of the pool. The blocks are approximately 2 feet above the pool surface. They are always the same height. So, once you learn it, it will always be the same.

As with any dive, the racing dive should be practiced only in the deep end of the pool for reasons of safety.

In a racing dive, you push off with your legs and arms and fling your arms out in front of you, launching your body into the air and then into the water in a streamlined position, angled down slightly at entry. Because of the push your legs get, you may go up a little with your hips and then down, but the focus should be on going as far out as you can and then getting into the water a foot or two below the surface and, finally, angling up to begin swimming the stroke.

If you are a competitive swimmer, your coaches will have you practice starts and turns often because these moves can be the difference between winning and losing close races.

The tricky part of racing dives for most beginners is keeping their goggles on during the dive. Goggles have to be tight. Some racers put their caps on over their goggles to help keep them in place.

Backstroke Starts

Performing the backstroke start properly is essential for competitive swimmers. As with everything else, there are techniques.

To do a backstroke start, you grab the bar under the starting block and put your toes against the wall, with your knees bent 90 degrees. You then pull your body up so that your head is almost touching the bar. You push off the wall with your legs and then arch your back as you throw your arms back, making a rainbow shape, and enter the water. Your hands enter first, followed by your head and the rest of your body, with your feet going in last. From there, a foot or two under the water, you begin your dolphin kick and angle up to the surface in a streamlined position to start the stroke.

Postal Swims

If you don't belong to a team but want to enter an event, try a postal swim. These are conducted several times a year by different swim clubs. You, or you and your friends if it is a postal relay, swim your times and mail in the results. People from all across the country—sometimes the world—enter postal swims.

WHAT'S FASTER, WHAT'S SLOWER

To go your fastest, keep these guidelines in mind:

- A halfway decent flip turn is faster than any open turn.
- A backstroke flip turn with underwater dolphin kicks is faster than a backstroke turn with a backstroke kick.
- A breaststroke open turn with a pullout is faster than one without the pullout.
- A butterfly turn with small dolphin kicks under the water after the push-off is faster than one without the kicks.
- The fastest stroke at the top level is freestyle, followed by butterfly, backstroke, and breaststroke.

JOINING A TEAM: AGE-GROUP TO MASTERS

While many swimmers are content swimming on their own, others prefer a shared experience and like the idea of having coaching when they swim.

Age-group swimming in the United States starts for ages 5–6 and goes through age 18. If you are a young swimmer looking for a club, USA Swimming lists many clubs as well as state associations. If you can't find a suitable one, call your local YMCA, which will have a swim program or know about local swim clubs.

USA Swimming
usaswimming.org
USA Swimming is the national governing body for the sport of swimming. It administers competitive swimming in accordance with the Amateur Sports Act. This website is a great place to find a club near you, to check

national and international time standards, and to find news about your favorite world-class swimmer.

Masters swimming is for anyone over the age of 18 who wants to swim with a team or a club. The ability levels vary from lap swimmers to former competitive swimmers. Every Masters group will tell you that it doesn't matter if you are not a serious competitor, and it's true. So, don't be intimidated by former competitive swimmers.

If you are over 18 and aren't swimming with a college team but still like to compete, Masters is for you. Likewise, if you are older and don't have competitive experience but want to enter meets, you'll be glad to know that there are age-groups for Masters events. So if you are 45, for example, you won't be swimming against someone who is 25. Masters age-groups are 5-year spans, 40 to 44 for instance, and there are age-groups up to 100. Several swimmers in their early nineties still compete in Masters meets.

Some Masters clubs just offer the opportunity to swim with fellow members, while other Masters swimmers like to enter meets and travel to compete nationally and internationally. In fact, a recent Masters long course national included more than 1,000 swimmers from 155 teams across the country. They represent the extremely serious swimmers who still like the excitement of competition.

To find a Masters group near you, check out the website for United States Masters Swimming (USMS), which lists Masters organizations in all 50 states, divided into eight geographic zones.

United States Masters Swimming (USMS)
usms.org
United States Masters Swimming is a national organization that provides organized workouts, competitions, clinics, and workshops for adults aged 18 and over. Programs are open to all adult swimmers (fitness, triathlete, competitive, and noncompetitive). The national organization is 35 years old and has 500 clubs in 53 regions throughout the United States. There are more than 42,000 Masters swimmers, ranging in age from 18 to over 100.

WHERE TO FIND GEAR

Unless you live in a large city with a good sports store, you may have some difficulty finding goggles, caps, kickboards, pull buoys, and assorted swim gear locally. There are several companies that have been around for a number of years and are reliable when it comes to shipping and providing good products. Here are a few places to try:

World Wide Aquatics
worldwideaquatics.com
Online and catalog orders of swimming gear. They also have free swimming workouts.

Swim2000
swim2000.com
Online orders of gear and workouts for five days a week, which are e-mailed to you for free.

Workouts from both of these groups have beginning levels that start at 3,000–3,200 yards, so if you are really a beginner, the smart thing to do is to divide them in half or even in thirds. Since 1,760 yards equals an actual mile and 1,650 is a "swimming" mile, these workouts are nearly two miles in length, which is really not a beginner level.

Keifer
kiefer.com
Another online and catalog company for all kinds of swimming gear.

CHAPTER 10

EXERCISES TO STRENGTHEN SWIMMING-SPECIFIC MUSCLES AND PREVENT INJURIES

Shoulder injuries are a major risk for swimmers. In addition, over time, swimmers develop a muscle imbalance in the upper body: the chest area gets disproportionately strong, because it's used to power most of the action in swimming. You'll see many swimmers with forward, rounded shoulders due to this condition.

This chapter describes simple exercises that target the muscles in the area of the shoulder blades and middle back, to help balance out the muscles in the back of the shoulders with those in the front.

You should begin all of the exercises with one set of 10 and gradually progress to three sets of 10. These exercises should be done *only three times per week* (e.g., Monday, Wednesday, Friday or Tuesday, Thursday, Saturday) to avoid injury due to overuse.

BICEPS CURLS AND TRICEPS PRESSES

These exercises are routinely used by many types of athletes and are especially helpful for swimmers because both muscles attach at the shoulder.

Biceps Curls

Begin with dumbbells in each hand and straight arms. Bring weights up toward shoulders by bending elbows. Then slowly lower the weights.

Triceps Presses

Bend over at waist, with one hand on a table for support and the other holding a dumbbell. Begin with elbow bent to a 90-degree angle at your side. Straighten your elbow out behind you and then slowly bend it back to 90 degrees.

ROWS

Seated rows, using a rowing machine, or standing rows with a pulley system as well as lying on your stomach with dumbbells work the middle of the back in the area between the shoulder blades. All of the exercises are to be done with both arms moving in a rowing or sawing motion simultaneously, squeezing shoulder blades together.

ROTATOR CUFF EXERCISES

The rotator cuff keeps the shoulder stable. It has four muscles that need to be strengthened. Following is a pair of exercises for external rotation and internal rotation. It is easy to do them with Therabands or dumbbells.

I am more concerned with external rotation because swimmers typically have a large set of chest muscles—pectoral and lats—responsible for internal rotation. Only two tiny muscles control external rotation.

- **External.** Use a light weight, 3 to 5 pounds at most. Lie on your side, with your elbow bent 90 degrees. Raise and lower the weight, keeping your elbow by your side.

- **Internal.** Stay on the same side, but change hands with the weight. Raise and lower the weight now with the other arm, keeping the elbow on the floor.

Y-T-I

This is sort of like the YMCA song that features making letter shapes with your arms, only you do it lying on your stomach on a weight bench. Using light weights, 1 or 2 pounds, lift both arms at the same time. First, extend your arms up and out as if you are making a Y. Repeat 10 times. Then extend your arms straight out to the side, with your thumbs pointed up, to form a T. Repeat 10 times. Finally, place your arms by your sides, as if you were finishing a freestyle stroke, with your thumbs pointed down and your pinkies up. Raise and lower your arms 10 times.

These three exercises work the back, the rotator cuff, and the back of the shoulder. It is one of the best series of exercises for anybody—swimmers or not. I do it with 3-pound weights, and it is a killer.

SCAPULAR (SHOULDER BLADE) DEPRESSIONS

The best way to describe this exercise is that it is the opposite of a shoulder shrug.

Swimmers have huge upper trapezius muscles, the ones for shrugging shoulders. This exercise works the lower trapezius muscles, which attach to the shoulder blades, and our goal is to balance the two muscles.

- You can use a lat pull-down machine, without much weight, pulling until your arms and elbows are straight and your hands are by your sides. Then shrug your shoulders with no elbow bend and push straight down.

- You can also do this exercise sitting in a chair with arms. Push yourself up so that your rear is off the seat and your arms are straight. Keeping your arms straight, lower yourself back toward the seat without bending your elbows. Then push yourself up without bending your elbows. This one is hard for people to do. You start with your shoulder blades high and then push them down.

This gets the muscles that work the shoulder blades to move the way they are supposed to move. It strengthens the lower trapezius to help equalize the strength of the upper and lower trapezius.

Swimmers with huge muscle imbalances end up with shoulder problems.

BALL DRILL

Put a small medicine ball on a table or other surface where you can place your hand on the ball and lean on it. Make tiny clockwise circles, moving your whole arm while pushing into the ball.

PUSH-UPS PLUS SHOULDER BLADE EXERCISE

You can do this exercise with regular or modified push-ups. Modified push-ups are from the knees. After you push up and your elbows are straight, squeeze your shoulder blades in and then out.

You can also do this on a bench-press machine by pushing the machine until your elbows are straight. From that position, squeeze your shoulder blades together and then apart.

Most people want to bend their elbows, but this exercise is a tiny motion. It is not going to feel as if you are doing much. These muscles are more for endurance. They are responsible for moving the shoulder blade every time you move your arm. So, this should be done without much weight. You don't have to lift a lot of weight just to move all day long.

PUSH-UPS

If you do not have shoulder problems, push-ups are OK, but they are tough on shoulders. One benefit of push-ups is that with your hands on the floor or ground, you work a larger group of muscles. You can try modified or knee push-ups, which are also good for the abdominals. Push-ups are just a good all-around exercise.

PECTORAL STRETCH

You learned the pectoral stretch, or doorway stretch, in Chapter 1. This is an important maneuver because swimmers tend to be tight in the chest area, which will pull the shoulders forward and give you rounded shoulders.

ADDITIONAL WORKOUTS

The 12 workouts in this chapter have directions for stroke, distance, number of repeats, and rest. They are designed to help you improve.

You can also purchase workout books or sign up for swimming workouts online. However, many of those are geared to very experienced swimmers. For instance, Swim2000 (swim2000.com) and World Wide Aquatics (world wideaquatics.com) have beginner workouts that start at about 3,200 yards, with times that are designed for competitive or former competitive swimmers. That will not be appropriate for you if you are just beginning. Swim Info.com has shorter workouts. Swim2000.com will e-mail you five workouts per week.

In some cases, though, you can adapt an advanced workout to fit your level of experience. For example, if you find workouts of appropriate length but with times that you are not able to perform, you can simply adjust the times to your own intervals.

Key
1. "1 × 25" means swim 25 yards one time of the specified stroke or drill. "4 × 25" means swim four lengths of 25 yards in the specified stroke or drill. "4 × 50" means four 50-yard swims. "4 × 100" means four 100-yard swims. And so on.
2. "Odd—free/even—choice drill" means swim the first freestyle and the second in your choice of stroke. For instance, "8 × 50 @ 20 seconds rest, odd—free/even—choice drill" means do eight 50-yard swims with 20 seconds of rest between each one, and swim the first,

third, fifth, and seventh freestyle and the second, fourth, sixth, and eighth using your choice of stroke.

3. "Repeat 4 times" means do the set you just swam four times in all. The same applies for all other repetitions. For instance: "2 × 50, 2 × 75, 2 × 100 @ 20 seconds rest, repeat 4 times" means to swim those in order with 20 seconds of rest between each, doing it four times in that order without taking a long rest—unless, of course, you absolutely can't go on.

4. "4 × 100 (25 kick/25 swim/25 drill/25 swim)" means to swim each 100 yards as 25 yards kick, 25 yards swim, 25 yards drill, and 25 yards swim—with the drill of your choice, unless specified—and to swim it four times. Do that for all directions of this type.

5. "Pull": Although we have not worked on pull as a technique in this book, after you learn the strokes, you can improve by isolating either the legs or the arms. We have isolated the legs using a kickboard. Pulling isolates the arm portion of the stroke and enables you to work on strengthening that part of your body more specifically. Because the action of swimming emphasizes the upper body, swimmers do a lot of pulling. To pull, use a pull buoy. Put it between your upper thighs to allow your legs to drift along behind you while you work your arms. You may find that your freestyle, for example, is faster or slower using a pull buoy, depending on the percentage of strength you are getting from your upper versus lower body or the strength of your kick.

6. "IM" stands for "individual medley" and means butterfly, backstroke, breaststroke, freestyle—in that order. "Reverse IM" means freestyle, breaststroke, backstroke, butterfly.

7. "Descend" means to get faster with each swim. For instance, "descend 1–4, 5–8, 9–12" means swim the first, fifth, and ninth slowly and get faster each swim until the fourth, eighth, and twelfth are all-out. Descend can be done for any distance and any stroke. It is a good way to work on learning speed.

WORKOUT 1

New Swimmers
Warm up: 4 × 50 free
@ 20 seconds rest

Experienced Swimmers
Warm up: 4 × 75 free
@ 20 seconds rest

All with 15 seconds rest:

|---|---|
1 × 25 fly kick underwater	Same
1 × 25 rocket butterfly	Same
1 × 25 fly (right arm)	Same
1 × 25 fly (left arm)	Same
1 × 25 fly (3 right/3 left/ 3 full strokes)	Same
1 × 25 fly (2 right/2 left/2 full)	Same
1 × 25 fly (1 right/1 left/1 full)	Same
1 × 25 fly	Same
6 × 50 kick @ 20 seconds rest (all with fins, on side)	8 × 50 kick @ 20 seconds rest (all with fins, on side)
4 × 100 @ 20 seconds rest (25 fly drill/75 free)	6 × 100 @ 20 seconds rest (25 fly swim/75 free)
12 × 25 @ 15 seconds rest (1 fly fast/3 free easy)	16 × 25 @ 15 seconds rest (1 fly fast/3 free easy)
Warm down: 1 × 100 easy (1,500)	Warm down: 1 × 100 easy (2,000)

WORKOUT 2

New Swimmers	**Experienced Swimmers**
Warm up: 1 × 200 free	Warm up: 1 × 300 free
8 × 50 @ 15 seconds rest (25 fly kick underwater/ 25 rocket fly)	Same
12 × 25 @ 15 seconds rest	16 × 25 @ 15 seconds rest

(Both: work on streamline and fast dolphin kicks to the surface and two fast strokes; then easy freestyle to the wall)

2 × 50 free @ 15 seconds rest	Same
1 × 25 fly (3 right/3 left/3 both) @ 10–20 seconds rest	Same

2 × 50 free @ 15 seconds rest	Same
1 × 25 fly (2 right/2 left/2 both) @ 10–20 seconds rest	Same
2 × 50 free @ 15 seconds rest	Same
1 × 25 fly (1 right/1 left/1 both) @ 10–20 seconds rest	Same
2 × 50 free @ 15 seconds rest	Same
1 × 25 fly swim @ 10–20 seconds rest	Same
Warm down: 100 easy (1,500)	Warm down: 100 easy (1,700)

WORKOUT 3

New Swimmers	**Experienced Swimmers**
Warm up: 4 × 75 free @ 15 seconds rest	Warm up: 4 × 100 free @ 15 seconds rest
8 × 25 @ 20 seconds rest (odd—rocket butterfly/even— kick underwater)	Same
4 × 75 @ 20 seconds rest	6 × 75 @ 20 seconds rest
(Both: fly kick with board and fins, going faster each 25)	
Three times through set:	*Four times through set:*
2 × 25 fly with fins @ 15 seconds rest	Same
1 × 50 easy free @ 15 seconds rest	Same
Two times through set @ 15 seconds rest:	
1 × 25 fly	Same
1 × 50 (25 fly/25 back)	Same
1 × 75 (25 fly/25 back/25 breast)	Same
1 × 100 (25 fly/25 back/25 breast/ 25 free)	Same
Warm down: 100 easy (1,700)	Warm down: 100 easy (2,050)

WORKOUT 4

New Swimmers	**Experienced Swimmers**
Warm up: 8 × 25 free @ 10 seconds rest	Warm up: 6 × 50 free @ 15 seconds rest
100 IM drill @ 15 seconds rest	Same, but repeat twice
100 IM kick @ 15 seconds rest	Same, but repeat twice
100 IM swim @ 15 seconds rest	Same, but repeat twice
4 × 75 free @ 20 seconds rest (descend 1–4)	4 × 100 free @ 20 seconds rest (descend 1–4)
2 × 25 fly @ 15 seconds rest	Same
2 × 25 back @ 15 seconds rest	Same, except decrease rest from 15 seconds to 10
2 × 100 free @ 30 seconds rest	Same, except decrease rest from 30 seconds to 20
2 × 25 breast @ 15 seconds rest	Same, except decrease rest from 15 seconds to 10
2 × 25 free @ 15 seconds rest	Same, except decrease rest from 15 seconds to 10
2 × 100 IM @ 30 seconds rest	Same, except decrease rest from 30 seconds to 20
Warm down: 100 easy (1,500)	Warm down: 100 easy (2,000)

WORKOUT 5

New Swimmers	**Experienced Swimmers**
Warm up: 1 × 200 free	Warm up: 1 × 300 free
1 × 300 free	1 × 400 free
8 × 50 @ 20 seconds rest (odd—free/even—choice drill)	8 × 75 @ 20 seconds rest (odd—free/even—choice drill)

All with 20 seconds rest:

1 × 200 free 70% effort	Same
2 × 25 easy free	Same
1 × 150 free 80% effort	Same
2 × 25 easy free	Same
1 × 100 free 90% effort	Same
2 × 25 easy free	Same
1 × 50 free 100% effort	Same
2 × 25 easy free	Same
Warm down: 100 easy (1,700)	Warm down: 100 easy (2,100)

WORKOUT 6

New Swimmers	**Experienced Swimmers**
Warm up: 1 × 200 free	Warm up: 1 × 300 free
6 × 50 free @ 15 seconds rest	8 × 50 free @ 15 seconds rest

One 100 of each stroke @ 20 seconds rest:

4 × 100 (25 kick/25 swim/25 drill/ 25 swim)	Same

One round of each stroke @ 15 seconds rest:

2 × 25 kick fast	Same
1 × 25 easy free	Same
1 × 75 drill (perfect technique)	Same

Three times through set:	*Five times through set:*
1 × 75 easy free @ 10 seconds rest	Same
1 × 25 fast free @ 20 seconds rest	Same
Warm down: 100 easy (1,900)	Warm down: 100 easy (2,300)

WORKOUT 7

New Swimmers
Warm up: 1 × 200 free

3 × 100 free @ 20 seconds rest

16 × 25 drill (IM order)
@ 15 seconds rest

1 × 100 free @ 15 seconds rest

2 × 75 breast @ 15 seconds rest

3 × 50 back @ 15 seconds rest

4 × 25 fly @ 15 seconds rest

10 × 50 kick choice @
15 seconds rest (25 easy/25 fast)

Warm down: 100 easy (2,000)

Experienced Swimmers
Warm up: 1 × 300 free

4 × 100 free @ 20 seconds rest

12 × 50 drill (IM order) @
15 seconds rest

Same

Same

Same

Same

Same

Warm down: 100 easy (2,400)

WORKOUT 8

New Swimmers
Warm up: 1 × 200 free

Twice through set (freestyle):

4 × 75 free @ 20 seconds rest

2 × 50 kick @ 10 seconds rest

2 × 50 drill @ 10 seconds rest

1 × 100 swim @ 15 seconds rest

Then:

8 × 75 free @ 30 seconds rest
(25 slow/25 med/25 fast)

1 × 100 easy

1 × 100 fast!

Warm down: 100 easy (2,300)

Experienced Swimmers
Warm up: 1 × 300 free

4 × 100 free @ 20 seconds rest

Same

Same

Same

12 × 75 free @ 30 seconds rest
(25 slow/25 med/25 fast)

1 × 100 easy

1 × 100 fast!

Warm down: 100 easy (2,900)

WORKOUT 9

New Swimmers	**Experienced Swimmers**
Warm up: 1 × 200 free	Warm up: 1 × 300 free
4 × 100 free @ 20 seconds rest	5 × 100 free @ 20 seconds rest

Twice through set:

4 × 50 IM order (25 kick/25 drill) @ 15 seconds rest	Same
1 × 200 free @ 20 seconds rest	Same

Then:

12 × 25 kick @ 15 seconds rest (descend 1–4, 5–8, 9–12)	Same
50 easy	Same
4 × 100 free (25 fast/75 easy) @ 20 seconds rest	8 × 100 free (25 fast/75 easy) @ 20 seconds rest
Warm down: 1 × 50 easy (2,200)	Warm down: 1 × 50 easy (2,800)

WORKOUT 10

New Swimmers	**Experienced Swimmers**
Warm up: 1 × 200 free	Warm up: 1 × 300 free
2 × 200 free @ 20 seconds rest	2 × 300 free @ 20 seconds rest

All with 15 seconds rest:

4 × 25 fly drill	Same
1 × 50 fly kick	Same
1 × 100 IM	Same
4 × 25 back drill	Same
1 × 50 back kick	Same
1 × 100 IM	Same

4 × 25 breast drill	Same
2 × 50 breast kick	Same
1 × 100 IM	Same
4 × 25 free drill	Same
2 × 50 free kick	Same
1 × 100 IM	Same

Pull (arms only, use pull buoy):

4 × 75 free (slow/med/fast) @ 20 seconds rest	6 × 75 free (slow/med/fast) @ 20 seconds rest
4 × 50 free (med/fast) @ 20 seconds rest	6 × 50 free (med/fast) @ 20 seconds rest
4 × 25 free (fast) @ 20 seconds rest	6 × 25 free (fast) @ 20 seconds rest
Warm down: 100 easy (2,300)	Warm down: 100 easy (2,900)

WORKOUT 11

New Swimmers	**Experienced Swimmers**
Warm up: 1 × 200 free	Warm up: 1 × 300 free
8 × 50 free @ 10 seconds rest	8 × 75 free @ 10 seconds rest
4 × 100 free @ 15 seconds rest (25 swim/25 kick/25drill/ 25 swim)	Same
12 × 25 drill @ 10 seconds rest (4 fly/4 back/4 breast)	Same
9 × 100 @ 20 seconds rest (descend 1–3 free, 4–6 IM, 7–9 free)	12 × 100 @ 20 seconds rest (descend 1–3 free, 4–6 IM, 7–9 free, 10–12 IM)
Warm down: 100 easy (2,300)	Warm down: 100 easy (2,900)

WORKOUT 12

New Swimmers	**Experienced Swimmers**
Warm up: 1 × 200 free	Warm up: 1 × 300 free
1 × 400 free	1 × 500 free
12 × 50 @ 15 seconds rest, all choice of stroke (odd—kick/even—choice drill)	Same
Pull, 4 × 150 free @ 20 seconds rest (descend 1–4)	Pull, 4 × 200 free @ 20 seconds rest (descend 1–4)
12 × 25 choice @ 10 seconds rest (2 fast/1 easy)	12 × 50 choice @ 10 seconds rest (2 fast/1 easy)
Warm down: 100 easy (2,200)	Warm down: 100 easy (2,900)

INDEX